LIVING LIFE

TO THE

FULLEST

Ζώντας τη ζωή στο Έπακρο

12 Life Lessons from a
Greek-American Businessman

PETER E. PREOVOLOS

INDIE BOOKS
INTERNATIONAL

ISBN 13: 978-1-957651-04-0
Library of Congress Control Number: 2022904213

Designed by Steve Plummer, SP Book Design
Sketch of Benjamin Swig (page 47) by Dennis Auth

INDIE BOOKS INTERNATIONAL˚, INC.
2424 VISTA WAY, SUITE 316
OCEANSIDE, CA 92054
www.indiebooksintl.com

11-16-22

Dearest Jacqueline

Starting today _ _ _ _ always.
Live life to the fullest. Life is complex with many
curves and ups and down. Keep a positive attitude in
Christ in your life and remember to always look
for humor in everything. Humor & laughter helps
smooth out the bumps and gives you that special
up lift to take the next step.

With Admiration

"If we let ourselves believe that man began with divine grace,
that he forfeited this by sin, and that he can be redeemed only
by divine grace through the crucified Christ, then we shall find
a peace of mind never granted to philosophers. He who cannot
believe is cursed, for he reveals by his unbelief that God has not
chosen to give him grace."

BLAISE PASCAL (1623-1662) FRENCH SCIENTIST, MATHEMATICIAN, PHYSICIST,
PHILOSOPHER, MORALIST, AND WRITER

Contents

Preface vii

Chapter 1   Life Lessons From A Greek-American Businessman. . . . 1

Chapter 2   The Family Settles In America 7

Chapter 3   Success In The Restaurant Business. 13

Chapter 4   My Parents Start Their Life Together. 19

Chapter 5   My Childhood 29

Chapter 6   Finding My Confidence 43

Chapter 7   College Days. 51

Chapter 8   First Jobs 61

Chapter 9   Career Development 67

Chapter 10 New Beginning: Alpha & Omega 77

Chapter 11 Alpha & Omega Growth Spurt 85

Chapter 12 The Birth And Growth Of PenChecks. 93

Chapter 13 Changing The World One Child At A Time 105

Chapter 14 The Family And FDF 143

Chapter 15 The Future 147

Appendix

    A   Acknowledgments. 153

    B   About The Author. 155

    C   Notes 157

    D   Index 159

Preface

"When you set out on your journey to Ithaca, pray that the road is long, full of adventure, full of knowledge."
C.P. CAVAFY, 20TH CENTURY GREEK POET

WHY DOES ANYONE want to write a book about their life experiences and their family? Partly out of ego, partly to be remembered, and partly to validate their life experiences.

Perhaps writing this book is a testament to my faith. In the Greek Orthodox tradition, at a funeral service you do not say, "I'm sorry for your loss" or "You have my deepest sympathies." Instead, you greet each other with the words, "Life to you, may their memory be eternal." What a beautiful way to express your feelings, and to express that life has an eternal quality.

On the one-year anniversary of a death and every year thereafter, the family holds a brief memorial service at the conclusion of the church service. They serve *koliva*, a mixture of boiled wheat with raisins, sugar, candy-coated almonds, and coconut with a frosting of powdered sugar that has been blessed. It is offered to all those who attended church that day. At the end of the memorial service, the congregation sings, "May their memory be eternal."

I can't think of a more fitting tradition or a more meaningful one. It keeps us connected not just to tradition, but also to our own life's compass and purpose. We remember the good and the not so good, taking a moment to reflect on the person's life and what they meant to us. Perhaps it offers us an opportunity to reflect on our own lives in relation to the one we are remembering.

Like those remembrances, writing this book has allowed me to reflect on my life's events, both good and not so good. It's allowed me to honor my parents and my ancestors, as well as all those who have influenced me during the journey.

As I move into my late seventies, I've had the opportunity to look back at how many people have inspired me. I hope my stories will inspire others. A person doesn't have to be a saint, a guru, a world-class athlete, or a scientist to inspire others. In fact, of the many people I've met and worked with over the years, it's been the regular guys, not the celebrities, who've often inspired me the most. They dug in, did their work, obeyed the law, and were good citizens, as well as good fathers, mothers, employees, and employers. They are the people who are my unsung heroes—and the backbone of this great country. I hope when I come to the end of my journey, my path will somehow resemble theirs.

Finally, a word about memories. Stories are passed down from one generation to the next. Over time, some stories grow, some diminish; some are embellished, others are modified. That doesn't mean the stories are wrong, but they have changed enough to hold essential truths, yet are told within new contexts, whether it be the moment, the current period of history, or the cultural and societal environment of the time. In all cases, I have done my best to stay true to the spirit of the stories in this book.

Most of all, I would like my grandchildren and their children and their children beyond to understand where they came from—culturally and philosophically. My prayer is that in knowing their past, they will have a clearer roadmap to their own futures.

PETER E. PREOVOLOS
SAN DIEGO, CALIFORNIA, 2022

CHAPTER 1

Life Lessons From A Greek-American Businessman

"Happy is the man who can say, on his deathbed,
'I got my money's worth out of this life.'"
TOM POULOS, MY FATHER-IN-LAW

THE MAIN MESSAGE of this book is this: live life to the fullest and avoid taking hard stands that only get in the way of living your life to the fullest.

Here are the twelve life lessons contained within these pages:

1. Don't take everything so seriously, as if it's the end of the world.

2. Learn to forgive. Do not allow hatred or animosity to rule your life; they are a poison that will deeply infect your very being.

3. Allow yourself to experience the moment and cherish it as a gift, good or bad.

4. There is something to be gained from each experience that enriches you in ways you may not realize.

5. Don't forget what it was like to be a child—and practice it every once in a while. It helps when you are raising your own children; it can be an equalizer. Recalling what it was like to be a child has also allowed me the pleasure and the gratification, along with the privilege, of working with young people.

6. Work your hardest but learn to leave work behind when the day is done. Learn to play and play hard and well.

7. For those of you not yet of marriageable age or those thinking about it, remember when that day comes it will be a joyous moment. Relish it, for it generally only comes once. Learn to be patient, and above all, work and communicate with each other about every subject you can think of. Hold nothing back, because it's what you hold back or are afraid to talk about that will prove to be a barrier to fulfilment and a happy and fruitful marriage.

8. Carve out plenty of time for each other. Marriage can be fun and most fulfilling, but its success depends on how well you learn to share your deepest thoughts, passions, and feelings with each other. Between the two of you, nothing should be sacred or a secret. But the things that are closely shared should stay with only the two of you.

9. When you believe you have found your soulmate, take advantage of the courting phase to get to know each other well. Learn each other's habits, likes, and dislikes, since such knowledge will be critical to a successful marriage, especially in your later years. Always remember to make time for each of you to have the freedom of self-expression; encourage it and praise it. It is healthy. I am sure I have not fully embraced this to the maximum, but I'm working on it.

10. When children come into the picture, they will change your lives. It will be up to the both of you to never let being a parent interfere with your relationship as husband and wife. It can make your lives a little more complicated, but it can and will be extremely rewarding if you two stay true to your commitment to each other and your new role as parents.

11. When it comes to your careers, it isn't so much what you have chosen to do as it is how you deal with it. Enjoy life, for we only get one tour of duty on this planet. Take advantage of all its magnificence.

12. Put a smile on your face at all times. It will do wonders for your spirit, and it keeps people guessing.

MY GREEK ANCESTRY

My Greek ancestors, the early Hellenes, introduced the world to democracy, philosophy, arts, and mathematics in a way few cultures can claim. Socrates taught us to seek truth, while Plato advanced the notion that we are all responsible for one another. Sophocles was one of the world's first playwrights, bringing us tales of Oedipus and Antigone. Euclid created the foundation for modern geometry. The ancient Greeks sailed to the edge of the known world, and the military exploits of Alexander the Great brought the ancient world's largest empire under Greek control.

Socrates once said, "Anybody can be a Hellene, by his heart, his mind, his spirit." But being Greek by blood means one's history runs deep. There is a devotion to family, church, and culture that ties the Greek community together, even today.

As the son of Greek immigrants, I've truly lived the American dream. But as time flies by, I've turned to my own past to understand the journey I've taken, and what still lies before me.

PREOVOLOS ROOTS

With limited access to genealogy records, I've traced my family roots back to Theodore Panagopoulos, a resident of the city of Mercovouni, Arcadia, in the Peloponnese region. Arcadia is described in the Catalogue of Ships in Book II of Homer's epic poem, *The Iliad*. In Homer's account, Agamemnon, king of Mycenae and commander-in-chief of the Greek army in the Trojan War, set sail for Troy from the Peloponnese.

Theodore's descendant, George Theodore, was born about 1800, near Neochorion, Tripoli. George fought alongside Theodoros Kolokotronis, hero of the Greek War of Independence of 1821, against the Turks of the Ottoman Empire. The Peloponnese peninsula was the scene of fierce fighting, and the Peloponnesians, including my ancestor George Theodore, played a major role. At the end of the war, George, my great-grandpa, left the army. He later married Thanna Zigouri. Unfortunately, we know very little about her.

It was during this war that the family name changed from Panagopoulos to Pirovolos. It is said the change came about because George was responsible for the army's gunpowder and flints, and Pirovolos was derived from a combination of the Greek words for *powder* and *fire*.

One of the sons of George Theodore Pirovolos was my paternal grandfather, John George, who moved from Mercovouni to Neochorion, Arcadia, Greece.

When John George was old enough to marry, his father worked on a marriage proposal for him. Up until about the 1960s, dowries were a major part of the matchmaking process. The bride's parents were responsible for the dowry and the bigger the dowry, the better the catch.

In this case, the bride's father was amenable to the match and offered a two-story farmhouse and its furnishings for the newlyweds. In addition, her dowry included a large acreage for farming.

My great-granddad, being a shrewd businessman and negotiator (or so he thought), couldn't pass up such an offer. On the day of the wedding, all of the paperwork was completed, and the celebration began.

In those times, it was not uncommon for such festivities to last for several days, with people from both villages attending. As the celebration came to a close, one by one, the villagers on the bride's side of the family left, taking a piece of the household furnishings with them. It turned out that many of the villagers on the bride's side had lent the bride's father the furnishings to make the dowry look more valuable. By the time the guests had departed, the only things remaining in the house were the bedroom furnishings.

My father, Nicholas John, was born in that house on February 13, 1895. All of his siblings were born in the bedroom, except for Dad, who was born in the kitchen because his mother had gone into labor so quickly.

CHAPTER 2

The Family Settles in America

*"A simple way to take measure of a country is to look
at how many want in and how many want out."*
Tony Blair, Prime Minister of the United Kingdom, 1997–2007

A MERICA EXPERIENCED THE "great wave" of immigration between 1870 and 1920, when more than twenty million people arrived here. Although we Greeks are among the world's earliest seafarers, it wasn't until America's colonial era that we set out for the New World. As early as 1763, English settlers in Florida noted that the climate and soil were naturally suited for crops like olives, grapes, and oranges— crops cultivated by the Greeks. By 1768, hundreds of Greeks, mostly from central Greece, Crete, Turkey, and Cyprus, were among some one thousand skilled workers who set sail from the Mediterranean bound for Florida. They mostly settled in New Smyrna, where conditions were harsh, and eventually many Greeks moved on to St. Augustine. Greek migration to the US increased in the 1890s and continued through the first two decades of the twentieth century, in part due to hardships caused by the Balkan Wars and World War I. By the end of the nineteenth century, nearly 15,000 Greeks had entered the US; by 1917, some 450,000 Greeks had arrived.

My grandfather dreamed of coming to America and bringing his children. He made many trips, each time bringing another child with him. In 1899, he brought his oldest son, Panayotis (Peter) John, whom I was named after. They spent the first seven years living in Chicago. Next came my Uncle George John, followed by Aunt Christina, and Uncle Constantine John (Gus). The only one of Dad's siblings who didn't come to America was his brother Athanasios, who begrudgingly stayed in Greece to run the family farm.

My dad, Nicholas John Preovolos, with my grandfather John George Preovolos in 1927.

Nicholas John, my father, was the last of the siblings to migrate to the US. He was born in 1895 near Tripoli in the village of Neochori. At fourteen years old, he boarded a steamer named the *SS St. Paul* bound for New York City. After a stop in Le Havre, France, the vessel arrived in the US at the Port of New York on Saturday, October 8, 1910.

Brothers Peter, George, Gus, and Nick all headed to California. Uncle Pete's 1910 passport application showed that he became a naturalized US citizen in 1904 and listed his occupation as a restaurant keeper. Dad and his brothers in the US eventually became owners of the Imperial Grill, one of San Francisco's finest and largest restaurants in its time. I guess running a restaurant was meant to be for the Preovolos brothers.

At some point during this period, our name changed once again, from Pirovolos to Preovolos, because Uncle Pete thought the new name would be easier for non-Greeks to pronounce.

One of the first things Dad did upon arriving in San Francisco was find people who could teach him English. Although his formal education never went past the third grade, he eventually spoke English like he was born here, and became a voracious reader. He also made a lifelong commitment to physical fitness, both habits I'm happy to say I inherited.

MILITARY SERVICE

When the US became involved in World War I, Dad and his brothers filed draft registrations: Dad in 1917; Pete and George in 1918; Gus, date unknown. It's curious that Dad listed himself as the sole supporter of his mother and father, because he was the youngest of the brothers. It was probably because Dad wasn't married, so his wages went home to Greece. On Dad's draft registration he was described as short, with a medium build, brown eyes, and black hair. His occupation was that of a restaurant keeper. On their draft registrations, George and Gus were each listed as cooks and Pete as a restaurant proprietor. All were employed at 1607-1609 Market Street, home of the original Imperial Grill.

Dad was inducted into the US Army on the thirteenth day of the month.

Interestingly, he was born on the thirteenth, spent only thirteen days in boot camp, the ship that took him across the Atlantic to France took thirteen days, and there were thir-

My dad served as a Private First Class in the US Army during World War I, stationed with the 347th Field Artillery.

teen ships in the convoy. Dad loved telling the story about how he wore a size seven shoe, but the only size the army could give him was a ten, so he filled the toes with newspapers. At least it wasn't a size thirteen! During his service in France, Dad never fired a shot. Uncle Gus ended up serving in the Navy, but neither Pete nor George was ever called up.

On May 29, 1918, while stationed at Camp Lewis, Washington, Dad filed a "petition for naturalization," which included foreswearing allegiance to Alexander, "King of the Hellenes." On June 1, 1918, after taking the oath required by law, he became a US citizen.

Dad's commanding officer during the war was Lewis Williams Douglas, who later became ambassador to the Court of St. James, and served two terms as Arizona's representative in the Seventieth through Seventy-Third US Congress. Douglas went on to become the president of Mutual of New York Life Insurance Company before returning to public service, including an assignment as America's ambassador to the United Kingdom.

Dad was the cook for all of the officers and usually managed to serve them bacon and eggs, a luxury in the French camps. Douglas used to love to brag about "little Nick's" ability to barter with the locals to obtain eggs and bacon.

Years later, Douglas became the chairman and director of the Southern Arizona Bank and Trust Company in Tucson, Arizona. During my college years, when Dad visited me in Arizona, we would walk over to the bank, ride the elevator up to the executive floor, and ask the receptionist if Mr. Douglas was in.

Dad would say, "Just tell him little Nicky, the guy who used to cook him bacon and eggs in World War I, is out in front."

Mr. Douglas was most gracious, saying, "None of the other officers and generals ever understood how I could have bacon and eggs every morning! Remind me, Nicky, how the heck did you do that?"

Dad's Dream

Dad always told us about an incredible incident that happened during his tour of duty in France. He awoke from a dream in the middle of the night. He was dreaming of meeting his brother Gus in France crossing a bridge. He didn't give it much thought, but several days later while crossing a bridge, who should he meet in the middle but his brother. Obviously, the emotions at that moment were very high. When Dad asked his brother what he was doing, he said he was looking for Dad, because the Germans had blown up the boat he was stationed on.

"Well," said Dad, "I bartered with the farm girls with chocolates. I'd give them American chocolates and they'd give me eggs and bacon." That was my Dad.

After the war, Dad returned to San Francisco and the Imperial Grill.

CHAPTER 3

Success in the Restaurant Business

*"To be successful, you have to have your heart in
your business and your business in your heart."*
THOMAS J. WATSON, SR., CHAIRMAN AND CEO OF IBM, 1914–1956

THE PREOVOLOS BROTHERS' restaurant, the Imperial Grill, was located at 1067-1069 Market Street, just around the corner from my parents' first apartment on McAllister Street.

The name "Imperial Grill" sounds like a Chinese restaurant, but it wasn't. The restaurant happened to be located next door to the Imperial Theater, which was successful, so they "borrowed" the name for the restaurant.

My cousin Louis "Troy" Preovolos, born several years before I was, remembered the restaurant well, and wrote:

> *Our housekeeper often brought us [Louis and his brother, John] to the restaurant, which was a paradise for two little boys to explore. Uncle Peter, always upstairs in the office working over the books, would give us a few menus and pencils, and directed us back downstairs to an end table, where we would draw pictures on the backs of yesterday's menus. Your father [Nick] wore a tuxedo with a white carnation and always stood at the front as greeter. He would hand gardenias to the lady guests and*

cigars to the men of importance who came from the city hall. The icebox was a walk-in room with furry rabbits hanging on the walls, all kinds of meats, birds, and animals, while in the kitchen my father [George] directed the activities. There was a beautiful area where the baker made trays of French pastries, cakes, and pies. Uncle Gus was in charge of salads.

OPENING THE IMPERIAL GRILL

It's hard to imagine what those days must have been like; I wish I could have been there. In its heyday, the Grill employed five executive chefs and served San Francisco's prominent politicians, along with its upper and middle classes—including some less-than-savory diners. A story was reported of a man and a woman who dined at the Grill and were later arrested for the kidnapping and murder of Father Patrick Heslin of Colma, California. One of the witnesses against the defendants was George Arestis, one of Dad's busboys.

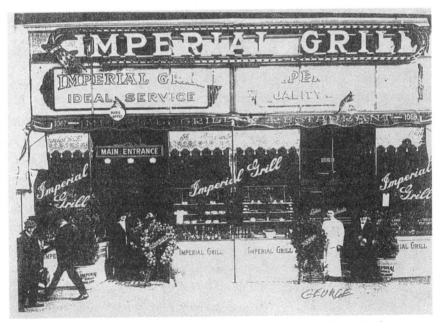

The Imperial Grill, circa 1914, was located at 1067-1069 Market Street. Uncle George Preovolos is pictured, as noted by Louis "Troy" Preovolos.

In those years, San Francisco had a vibrant Greek community; in fact, it has the distinction of being one of the oldest Greek-American communities in the US. My dad and uncles were prominent citizens.

Although the earliest Greek immigrants were gold miners and railroad laborers without families or long-term ties, many Greeks of Dad's era were drawn to San Francisco thanks to its reputation as a leading commercial, financial, and cultural center. We Greeks have a sense of pride about our financial independence and business ownership, so the city's booming commerce and trade were a good fit for us. By 1927, a *Greek Business Guide and Directory* listed nearly 200 café and restaurant owners.

In 1915, they expanded the restaurant, moving to Jones Street and Golden Gate Avenue. The Hibernia Bank was on the corner of Jones and Market, and the Grill was next door. The brothers spent $150,000 building a two-story, L-shaped restaurant. Though the Grill has been closed more than seventy years, the restaurant space was still there, with the original mosaic floor. As fate would have it, the property was being used for some time as a soup kitchen—back to its roots, feeding people. However, the building was demolished in 2016 and replaced with a new multi-story edifice.

Uncle Pete was somewhat of a local celebrity. With his seventh-grade education, he was the most educated of the brothers. Because most of the Greeks in San Francisco were uneducated, they came to Pete for advice. Most had left farms in Greece, hoping for a better life in the "promised land." I can remember, as a little kid, listening to some of the immigrants saying that they thought the streets in the US were lined with gold. Fortunately, like most Greeks of that era, they didn't shy away from hard work. When they ran into a problem or needed help reading a document, they came to Pete.

My Dad was on the receiving end of Uncle Pete's advice more than once, and in some cases, it was probably more like an ultimatum than friendly advice. Dad told me about meeting an Irish woman with whom he was enamored. But Pete and Dad's other brothers wouldn't hear of him getting serious about her because she wasn't Greek. Dad was forced to break off the relationship. Uncle Peter was concerned and began to search for a bride for my dad. He and Uncle Andrew Kokas worked together to put a plan in motion. It led to the arranged marriage between my dad and Fofo Touloumis, my mother.

I'm proud to say that the Preovolos brothers left quite a legacy in San Francisco. Pete, George, Gus, and Dad had managed, as immigrants, to build one of the largest restaurants in the city. They achieved a status in both the Greek and American communities that was unheard of for people with their background.

THE END OF AN ERA

The Imperial Grill flourished from 1907 until it closed its doors in 1933, six months before the repeal of Prohibition. A victim of the Great Depression, it closed before I was born. Uncle Peter died in 1930, heartbroken to see the end of the restaurant approaching and what the Great Depression had done to the business they had built.

The restaurant initially closed in 1933. Dad later reopened it and managed to keep the business going for a while, despite the prohibition against alcohol. Dad said more than once that if the repeal had happened six months earlier, the family would probably still be in the restaurant business.

Dad had a list of everyone he owed money to, and over time, he paid off everyone. It took him several years, but he did it. Dad liked the fact that he could look you in the eye and say, "I don't owe you anything. I had an obligation. I did it."

With the final closing of the restaurant, the family began going in different directions. Uncle Gus went to work in sales for Sterling Furniture Co., hardly making enough money to stay afloat. His wife, Vaselike (Aunt Bessie), went to work as a seamstress at Livingston Bros., a high-end women's department store. She managed to save enough money from her wages to prevent foreclosure on their home. Uncle Gus and Aunt Bessie had one child, Effie. Following the death of Uncle Gus in 1946, Aunt Bessie married Nick Lomis, an attorney from the East Coast who moved to California to set up a practice.

My mother started working at Weinstein's Department Store to help make ends meet after the restaurant closed. Owner Isadore Weinstein had been a customer of the Imperial Grill. The money my mother earned helped my dad start his liquor business on Townsend Street. The startup cost was $250.

Uncle Peter's wife, Kaliope, became a widow shortly after the first closing of the restaurant. Kaliope and Uncle Pete had two sons, John and Jim. Uncle Peter left her $50,000 in cash, a home that was paid off, and a gravesite purchased by the Imperial Grill. He and his close friend, Black Jack Jerome, one of San Francisco's colorful Greek citizens, had decided to buy gravesites next to each other. Kaliope went on a few years later to marry Mr. Daldos, a grocer of Greek ancestry.

Tragedy struck the Preovolos family with the loss of Uncle George's wife, Efthimia, who died from a burst appendix at the age of twenty. She left behind their two young children, John and Louis. With the death of his wife and the closing of the restaurant, Uncle George moved into a one-bedroom apartment with his sons. Emma G. Revell served as their beloved nanny and housekeeper for twenty-five years. A religious woman of Pentecostal faith, Emma kept her own home in the Richmond District of San Francisco. My cousin Louis recalls that my mother, Fofo, helped Emma during those years.

Uncle George and his friend, A.K. Thanos, had a reputation of being *men about town*, spending money on horse racing and women. A.K. Thanos would go on to be one of my dad's biggest competitors in the wholesale liquor distribution business.

CHAPTER 4

My Parents Start
Their Life Together

"A man without ethics is a wild beast loosed upon this world."
ALBERT CAMUS

MY MOTHER'S FAMILY

I WISH I KNEW as much about Mom's family as I do about Dad's. Mom, Fotini Doris Touloumis (called Fofo, meaning *light*), was born in Constantinople (now Istanbul), Turkey, but she was of Greek heritage. In April 1915, at the age of five, Mom traveled on the SS *Athinai*, sailing from Patras to New York with her mother and sisters.

My maternal grandmother was named Despina Touloumis. Her children, besides my mother, were Erasmia, who was eight years old in 1915 and went by the name of Irene; brother Sokratis, age six; and sister Epistimi, known as Sophia, age two. After

My mother, Fofo Preovolos, wearing a pearl necklace given to her by her father.

searching the records at Ellis Island, I learned that Mom's dad, Manuel John Touloumis, had arrived in the US on June 19, 1914, aboard the *Corcovado*. He was from Ganohora, Turkey, in the region of Thrace.

According to a 2015 blog entry from Father John Constantine describing his 2010 visit to his ancestral village of Millo, in the Ganohora region:

"I was going back to the village where my great-grandparents were forced to leave around 1912–1913 after the region suffered an earthquake. The Ottoman Turkish government thought it best that the inhabitants of the area be forced to leave. Of course, this was the beginning of the policy that resulted in the forced exchange of Greeks and Turks in 1922."

One of the few things I know about Mom's family is that they came to America because the Turkish government confiscated their land and nearly all their

My mother is twelve years old in this 1922 photo with her father, Manuel Touloumis. She is wearing her first dress.

wealth. What little money the Turks didn't take, a few gold coins, was smuggled out of Constantinople. The family legend is that the coins were secreted in Sophia's diaper.

Irene (Erasmia) later married a man named Hagi Kyriacou Asimidis Constantine, whose first name, Hagi, means "one baptized in the Jordan River." The family stories tell us he left Greece to avoid the draft, somehow making it to England. He became a naturalized US citizen under the name James Constantine. He and Irene had three children: Betty, Libby, and Jim. They settled in Los Angeles and developed a thriving candy business under the name Libby's Candy. They were later forced to change the name because of a suit brought by Libby's canned goods. The plant was located in Inglewood, a suburb of Los Angeles.

Mom's mother gave birth to one more child, who died shortly after being born. This took place during the influenza epidemic. The Spanish influenza epidemic also took my grandmother Despina's life.

Sophia married Nicholas Vardas and they had two sons, Leo and Chris. Sophia had a difficult, and at times, sad life and marriage, although both her sons were talented pianists and bright academically. Their father, Nicholas, was an outstanding violinist. Chris moved to Portland, Oregon, where he resides today. The older son, Leo, was considered an expert in Einstein's theory of relativity and was a graduate student at UC Berkeley. He went on to establish a career at the Jet Propulsion Laboratory (JPL), eventually retiring from there.

Fofo Preovolos

After the marriage of Irene's two daughters, Irene divorced Kyriacou. She moved to the East Coast, eventually remarried and had a son, whose name is Chuck Troupe. Shortly after the birth of her son, she married Herb Ankrom. She also started her own business offering services to Pennsylvania convalescent care facilities. Irene built that business into a major enterprise, and then sold it to a large organization. My aunt was a shrewd businesswoman who contributed significantly to the building of two successful companies during her lifetime.

GRANDMA MABEL SHAPES MY LIFE

After Despina died, apparently my grandfather, Emanuel John, was a basket case, beside himself with grief. For a period of time, he farmed all their children out to relatives. Eventually he married Mabel, a waitress who worked for him in his restaurant and ice cream parlor, located on Telegraph Avenue in Oakland.

Mabel was partly descended from the Cherokee North American Indians. She was born with a cleft lip and because of that spoke with a slight lisp, which almost sounded like an accent. She was the epitome of a true frontier woman: strong-willed, tough as nails, and determined. There was nothing she couldn't do if she put her mind to it. Probably the best way to describe her is she was like an Annie Oakley. Mabel could shoot, and at one stage in her life she chewed tobacco, smoked cigars, was a good farmer, and rode a motorcycle.

Mabel's son from her first marriage became a highly respected mining engineer. Sadly, he died in an auto accident. Attempting to jump from a car heading off a cliff, as he was jumping, the door of the car pinned his leg, dragging him over the cliff with it. His funeral was the first one I ever attended. I was seven years old.

Grandma Mabel raised chickens; she would go into the chicken coop, grab whichever chicken she wanted to serve for dinner, and twirl it around by the neck until it broke. After gutting it, she would immerse it into a kettle of boiling water for a short time to make plucking the feathers easier.

Mostly, I remember Mabel for the love and care she showed and the interest she took in expanding my world. When I was around nine years old, she took me downtown to San Francisco via the streetcar. We were going to learn about the exciting world of stamp collecting. She bought me my first stamp album and the Scott Standard Postage Stamp Catalogue, both of which I still have.

She also took me to the movies; I have a vivid memory of going with her to see the *Phantom of the Opera*, starring Claude Rains. I had nightmares for many months afterward. Doing those kinds of things was just Mabel's nature. I was so fortunate to have had her in my life.

We had a tintype photograph of her and her entire family, standing next to the covered wagon they used to come to California. Her father was dressed in a Native American headdress and the rest of the family was dressed in traditional clothing made of animal skins. Unfortunately, that photo was stolen from us.

One final anecdote about Grandma Mabel was that she smoked unfiltered Camel cigarettes, using a paper cigarette holder, which was popular in those days.

I would often ask Mabel to stop smoking.

"See, Peter, I am cutting down," she would say. "I am cutting each cigarette in half, so I'm only smoking half as much as I used to."

She still managed to finish a pack a day.

MY PARENTS' MARRIAGE

When she was young, my mom spent a period of time in a Catholic convent, probably no more than a year. From there she went to Modesto, living with other relatives, and then finally to San Francisco to live with the family of her uncle, Andrew Kokas. Those were still the days of arranged marriages, and in 1929, her Uncle Andrew told her she was going to marry Nick Preovolos. My Uncle Pete and Andrew were close friends, and together they decided Nick was going to marry Fofo.

Mom and Dad were married on June 29, 1929. She was seventeen years old, and Dad was thirty-four. A big age difference was not uncommon in the days of arranged marriages. In fact, there was a thirty-year age difference between my mother-in-law and father-in-law.

My cousin Louis wrote this recollection of my mother and father:

> I first met Aunt Fofo at the Imperial Grill when Uncle Nick introduced her as our new aunt. My brother and I fell in love with her, as she was not only beautiful, but she spoke English. My brother and I held candles at the wedding of Uncle Nick and Aunt Fofo, as we were still children.

My mother was good with money, and on top of it, was beautiful, creative, charming, and a little narcissistic, some might say. Mom loved to copy fashions from renowned designers. If she saw a Dior creation, for example, she could make the pattern, cut, and sew it. Of course, everyone thought she had *a real Dior*. Mom loved that people thought she bought the latest fashions. She was very clever with designing clothes. If a garment could be made by sewing, knitting, or crocheting, she could make it, including handbags, lace doilies, afghans, socks, and sweaters. I still remember the knit suits she made for herself and the sweaters and socks she made for my brother Ted and me.

If my sense of ethics and business savvy came from my dad, I definitely inherited a sense of style and social grace from Mom. She was creative in everything she did, whether it was needlepoint, decorating, or cooking. Simply put, Mom made the world more beautiful. Not only could she make something, but it would also be presented with class and beauty.

Mom was also a whiz at decorating and used whatever materials she could find to sew curtains and cover orange crates for furniture. My cousin Louis said he remembers how beautiful the "furniture" had been in their apartment. Mom's beauty, youthfulness, and talent made her a hit with all my cousins, who were not much older than she was.

Mom was also a gifted painter and an outstanding cook. She learned from the best: Uncle George and Uncle Gus of the Imperial Grill! She was phenomenal in the kitchen and there wasn't anything she couldn't make, no matter how complicated. In later years, Mom could put on a dinner party fit for a king.

Before and during their early married life, Dad worked at the Imperial Grill, which he loved. But he had a number of other interests, including wrestling. Dad was a light featherweight wrestler weighing in at 120 pounds. He was undefeated in his class for several years, while wrestling for San Francisco's prestigious Olympic Club.

Between 1930 and 1939, Dad, weighing 125 pounds, also refereed professional wrestling matches for five dollars a night. In fact, the night my brother was born, Dad was climbing into the ring in San Jose to referee a match featuring "Man Mountain Dean," a native New Yorker who had earlier wrestled under the moniker Hell's Kitchen Bill-Bill. The contest between Man Mountain and Pat McClary of Ireland was over in four and a half minutes, when Man Mountain "smacked

McClary and then dropped his full 325 pounds of suet on the horizontal figure," according to an article in the San Francisco Chronicle.

Dad refereed another match that night. Reporter Alan Ward wrote that Referee Preovolos "almost stole the show when he pulled his belt and almost 'strangled' Pat Fraley [wrestler] into submission, after the latter made a few ungentlemanly passes in his direction.

They had to bring in the police to escort Dad out of the arena that night. He loved telling the story of how the women in the crowd spat at him and tried to kick him on his way out.

Refereeing a fight between Baron Ginsberg and Ganson Velcoff, Dad tries to grab Ginberg's mustache to break his illegal hold on Ganson.

AFTER THE IMPERIAL GRILL

After the restaurant closed, Dad went to work as a salesman for Glaser Brothers, which was the largest wholesale cigar and tobacco company on the Pacific coast at the time. The company was started in San Francisco in 1888 as a tobacco storefront and went on to serve many small, mostly ethnic stores. After generations of ownership, the Glaser family sold the business, which operates today as Core-Mark, one of the largest marketers of supplies for the convenience retail industry in North America.

I think it was during that time when Dad made a point of learning a few phrases in Norwegian, Russian, Italian, Chinese, and Japanese as a sign of respect to the immigrant shop owners who bought his products. All his work for Glaser Brothers was on a commission basis.

After a period of time, Mr. Glaser called him in and told him he had a great opportunity—instead of him relying on a commission, the company would guarantee him a steady paycheck by putting him on a straight salary. That way, said Mr. Glaser, Dad's income would be stable. The company made this offer not out of generosity or appreciation, but because Dad was making more on his commissions than any other salesman. Feeling like he was being taken advantage of (a terrible situation for an integrity-based guy like my dad), he quit the company.

During this time, Mom was working in Weinstein's basement as a cashier, saving every penny she could. After Dad quit working at Glaser Brothers, he had the opportunity to open a liquor distribution business. Since Prohibition was over, getting into that business was one of the best decisions Dad could have made. The problem was he didn't have the $250 to buy a license to distribute liquor.

I can only imagine how shocked he was when Mom pulled a coffee can off the shelf and emptied all her savings onto the kitchen table—a total of $252 and pennies. Dad didn't know it, but every day Mom walked to work instead of taking the streetcar, often skipping lunch so she could put the money away for a rainy day. The rainy day had come, and Dad purchased his liquor license.

We Greek men have a high regard for women because of the sacrifices they are willing to make for their husbands and families, probably due in part to stories like this, of Mom saving for a rainy day so Dad could get ahead. My father would tell my brother and me, just as we started noticing girls, that when you date a girl, you must respect her as if she was your sister. It certainly set a standard and sent a strong message that you don't take advantage of a woman.

In the Greek Orthodox Church, women are held in high esteem within the family. While the man may be the face of the family, the woman is the power behind the throne. In our home, as is typical in Greek households, Mom made all of the decisions about the home. If she wanted to move the furniture, she moved it. If Mom didn't want something to happen in the home, it didn't. In my own household today, my wife is the keeper of the home and if something is going to affect the life of the family in the home, she plays a role equal to mine in making a decision.

In the Greek Orthodox Church tradition, during the marriage ceremony, the couple is crowned as king and queen of their kingdom. The union of a man and a woman isn't about who will dominate, but how to build and protect your kingdom.

Our church elevates Mary the Theotokos (Greek for "God-bearer") to such an extraordinary position because she was the mother of Christ. Mary deservedly belongs there, but she also represents women everywhere. If you want somebody to emulate, can a woman or man find a better role model? In the Greek Orthodox faith, the honorific name for the Virgin Mary is Panayia, *Pan* meaning "all" and *agios* meaning "saint or holy." I am proud to carry the masculine representation of her name, Panayoti. What a standard to try to live by. I am still trying.

CHAPTER 5

My Childhood

*"Train up a child in the way he should go; and
when he is old, he will not depart from it."*
PROVERBS 22:6

I WAS BORN ON July 2, 1939, during a time when America was recovering from the Great Depression.

Starting at about eighteen months of age, I was in and out of hospitals. I first came down with pneumonia, then double pneumonia. After my parents brought me home from the second episode, within forty-eight hours my head puffed up and they rushed me back to the hospital. Within twenty-four hours in the hospital, my head broke out with boils as a reaction to all the medication I had been given. I had curly hair, which they had to shave; my hair never grew back curly again. Shortly after this episode, I began suffering from asthma and eczema, which bothered me for the next twelve years.

The eczema broke out on the back of my legs and arms so badly that I was frequently admitted to the hospital, including once when I was only five or six years old. I was placed in a metal-frame hospital crib, with both my hands and feet tied to the frame to prevent me from scratching. I don't remember what medication they used to treat the eczema, but it was paste-like and smelled like tar. To this day the smell of tar takes me right back to my days in the hospital. In fact, Neutrogena shampoo brings back memories of that scent: perhaps it's formulated from similar base ingredients.

After years of doctors and hospitals, my parents took me to the Sansum Medical Clinic in Santa Barbara, the first multi-specialty clinic on the West Coast, which had a reputation much like the Mayo Clinic. Incidentally, 2021 marks the one hundredth anniversary of Sansum Clinic. We took the train to Santa Barbara, where the clinic ran me through a series of some 2,000 allergy scratch tests, along with a battery of other tests. When it was all over, we sat in the doctor's office for a final consultation and to review all the test findings. The doctor told my parents by the time I was twelve years old, I would outgrow the problem. Talk about the power of suggestion. When I was twelve, all those medical issues went away and I didn't have problems with eczema again until my freshman year in college during final exams.

GROWING UP GREEK

I look back on my childhood and know I was one of the luckiest kids ever. Growing up the son of immigrants, I learned how to live in two worlds. I used to say to my friends that Greek-American kids lived two lives: one Greek and the other American. However, my Greek heritage always took precedence. My religion, ethics, attitude, and cuisine were Greek, but I experienced them as an American. My father, and most immigrants I encountered in my early years, loved this country and truly believed it was a privilege to be an American. They loved to work and contribute to the country that gave them the opportunity to be successful.

Dad constantly reminded us of how lucky we were to be Americans. In those years, the Greek community of San Francisco was close, and our family was constantly going to people's homes, entertaining at our home, or attending baptisms, weddings, and funerals. There was always something going on in the community. We were a village within a very large city. This allowed us to move freely back and forth with ease, never missing a beat. If there was a party at someone's home, you could rest assured there would be plenty of Greek food and lots of Greek dancing.

My parents entertained a great deal. Mom was an extraordinary cook who loved getting compliments from our guests. Other men would tell my father, "You are the luckiest man to be married to such a great cook." Mom was also strikingly beautiful. People said she resembled Elizabeth Taylor, which Mom loved!

Many times, my dad would call home at 3:00 p.m. and say he was bringing a client home for dinner. Mom would whip up a meal that knocked your socks off. Invariably, the guest would ask how she did it on such short notice. Mom was simply a great cook with a flair for entertaining. Something I will always remember is how easily she could throw a party. It didn't matter if the party was for five people or one hundred—the guests marveled at her dinner parties. She was proud of her creations and Dad was even prouder. Mom was often called on to chair fundraisers for the church and Greek community.

In 1949, when I was ten, my parents built their dream home at 50 Encanto Way in San Francisco. It was a three-story house with fourteen rooms and two sundecks. It had a thirty-three by fifteen-foot rumpus room with a fireplace. That room had a gorgeous professional bar, the type you would find in a first-class restaurant, with all the requisite tools. The room was designed to host large parties.

When we had parties, my brother and I tended bar. While we were growing up, the bar was never locked from us kids. In fact, if there was wine on the table, we were offered a small taste. My brother and I never viewed alcohol as something forbidden, and I think that's why we never considered it a big deal. Our friends tried to sneak it from their parents. In most households, liquor was kept under lock and key or the parents put marks on the bottles to measure the amount of alcohol in them. My friends bragged about drinking from the bottle and then putting water in to bring it back up to the mark. For us, it was never forbidden fruit.

However, Mom reminded us of how dangerous it was if any of our friends were caught drinking alcohol in our home; it would put

Dad out of business. We never took any alcoholic beverages from the house, even though it would have been easy to do so.

LESSONS FROM MY FATHER

Dad loved to tell people he was in the spirit uplifting business. It was a play on words that was true, literally and figuratively.

Dinner at our house was a time when the entire family ate together. It was a time for all of us, no matter how young, to engage in conversation. Dinner table conversations revolved around politics, religion, school, our behavior, and who we were as Greeks. During those conversations, we were taught to respect everyone and that we were not better than anyone else, just different because of our heritage. My parents wanted us to understand our cultural background and history, but we were taught to seek the beauty in other people and to try to better understand their cultures and backgrounds.

Most of our history discussions were about ancient Greece, unless the subject turned to what we endured under Turkish rule, and how we kept our language and faith alive. Being Greeks, we found a way around the school and church closures, doing everything at night so it would be hidden away from the Turks.

One time I said the Turks were bad.

Dad's take on this was: "How do you think people might have felt when Alexander the Great was conquering the known world and disrupting their lifestyle?"

Dad said we don't condone what took place, but we do pray for enlightenment.

Dad always tried to instill the right behavior in us. He taught us the importance of being polite, that everyone's mother is good (but yours is the best), and that every religion is good (but ours is the best).

Dad would say things like, "Would you deny your mother? Then don't deny your church."

We went to Greek school every Wednesday afternoon and to church every Sunday. We never missed a Greek Orthodox religious holiday.

For the Greek Orthodox, Pascha (Easter) is our most sacred holiday. Every Sunday during my grandparents' lifetime, we went to San Mateo and visited them after church. I remember the victory garden they had during the war years. It was magnificent, filled with all kinds of vegetables and sunflowers.

Dad loved the church, but if he saw the bishop or priest do something he didn't agree with he would be the first one to speak up. At one Good Friday service, the donation tray was being passed among the congregation. My dad went up to receive the blessing from the bishop.

"You know, Your Grace," he said, "I was at a funeral the other day, and can you imagine, they were passing a tray."

"No, don't tell me that!" the bishop replied.

Dad started laughing, and the bishop said, "Oh my, I certainly walked into that."

That was my dad's way of pointing out that Good Friday represents Christ's funeral. During a most sacred moment in the life of the church, we had to stop and pass a collection tray while supposedly contemplating the significance of Christ's sacrifice.

Dad instilled in us an amazing work ethic. He told us that when you work for someone, if you are supposed to be there at 8:00 a.m., arrive at 7:30 a.m. If quitting time is 5:00 p.m., leave at 5:30 p.m., and never look at the clock.

"You must give a full measure of yourself; if not, it's like stealing from the boss," according to my dad.

Dad was also big on lessons about the importance of saving. When I had my first real job delivering papers, he told me for every dollar I saved he would match it, but for every dollar I withdrew from savings I owed him a dollar plus interest. With rules like that, I thought twice before spending my money.

Being respectful to teachers and elders was also important to Dad. If we were reprimanded at school, regardless of whether we were right or wrong, we got worse at home. He never spanked us (I think he was afraid of hurting us), but he did believe in what I call "learning lectures." Mom, on the other hand, would come at us with a spoon, a coat hanger, or whatever was handy. If she complained about anything openly to my dad, it was when my brother and I misbehaved.

My brother Ted was the one punished most often. Mom and Ted were so much alike that they were constantly in conflict. Ted was, and still is, a strong-willed individual, and Mom never seemed to be able to control him. The last time she used the soup spoon, she broke her favorite one on him.

As my dad became more affluent, things actually got a little harder on me. We had a maid, Katina, who was an immigrant from Russia via Shanghai. Throughout my teen years. Katina was not allowed to make our beds, pick up our clothes, or iron them. Dad insisted we learn how to wash and iron our clothes and perform simple sewing tasks. I rebelled at this.

Dad would say one day I'd be married and what would I do if my wife was sick or about to give birth?

"Someone has to step in and help and it had better be you."

I would respond, telling him, "That's what a wife is for."

That comment never sat well with him. He was way ahead of his time, quite enlightened. He was not a believer in women's liberation (for example, he didn't want Mom to work outside of the home and family when we were growing up), but he did believe we all have responsibilities, and from time to time they must

The Gift of Tolerance

I learned about integrity and tolerance early on. At the dinner table, my mother and father would impart to my brother and me the basic principles of life:

Do good.

Do the best you can.

Try hard.

Be respectful to everybody.

Do not discriminate.

Mom and Dad especially felt that the early immigrants to America, whether they were Italian, Chinese, Russian, Irish, or whatever nationality, all deserved our respect.

America is the most sophisticated, exciting quilt ever made, with human beings from all over the world and from every walk of life. The revolution in the US was successful largely because our founders had a vision, a purpose, and a magnificent goal: freedom. Immigrants who come from places where they hated their next-door neighbor or people from a neighboring country have come here and learned to coexist, even thrive, alongside those same neighbors.

be shared. I must admit with shame I haven't always lived up to that standard, but I am trying.

We never received an allowance for doing chores around the house because we were expected to help out. It was our responsibility for the privilege of living in a nice home and for being properly clothed and educated. If we wanted something, we sought approval for buying it. We always had to explain what it was for and why we thought we needed it.

If Dad didn't give us the money, he'd say, "If it's that important to you, find a job and make some money, and then see how important you think this purchase is to you."

Learning to cook was also a must; a Greek male who can't cook is a rarity. Greek men of my generation won't go hungry, and all three of my sons are very good cooks.

Dad taught me a lot about business, ethics, and responsibility, but some of his best lessons were about generosity. In spite of going through the Depression and experiencing the loss of the family business, he always told us to be generous and never short-change charity or the church. He liked to say God's pocket is bigger than ours, so be generous. I loved that phrase and when I had children of my own, I told them the same thing.

ON THE FARM IN LODI, CALIFORNIA

I was lucky to spend part of my childhood on two farms. The first farm was in Lodi, California. It was owned by Uncle Barba Simos, a Greek Orthodox monk who was a relative of my father's. He came to America with several other monks to escape religious persecution in Greece, and initially settled in Arkansas, where they built their monastery, which still exists today.

Apparently, Barba Simos had a falling out with the group, so they gave him his share of the profits and he went to California, where he bought a one-hundred-acre vineyard and farm. Our family spent all of our summers there through the 1930s and 1940s. I went there until I was about eight years old.

I have fond memories of the Lodi farm because it was a gathering place for the relatives and friends during the summer. The adults hunted dove and rabbit together. One day they drove out for dove hunting in a Model T Ford, taking my brother Ted with them. When they returned from hunting, the car wouldn't start, so they decided to go back out and continue hunting. Ted, the contrarian, stayed in the car and as fate would have it, he got the car started and drove it back to the farmhouse. Doing that kind of thing was typical of my brother.

On the farm, my mother would cook up a storm and do a lot of canning with her best friend, Minnie Frangotis. Minnie was a practicing registered nurse, and her husband was a shoe cobbler who owned several hundred acres of almond and walnut trees in the area. In later years, Minnie was a godsend when Mom had a hysterectomy. She came to San Francisco and cared for Mom at the hospital, and for a while, at home.

It was on the Lodi farm that an all-black cat became my first pet. When we left that summer, I was sad because Mom and Dad wouldn't let me bring the cat home. All year, I thought about the cat and couldn't wait until I saw him again. When summer came and we returned to the farm, I learned the cat had been hit by a truck and died. I think that was my first lesson about sadness, one that wouldn't leave me for a long time.

Memories of my Uncle Barba Simos are far happier. He made wine for all of his friends, although I can't remember if I ever tried it. My uncle had a few unique characteristics, including taking at least two hours to eat his meal. And if he was served chicken, he ate everything, including the bones. As a young child, I watched him in absolute amazement. I can still see him brushing his teeth by pouring salt on his finger and rubbing his teeth and gums.

A monk by profession and training, he read the Bible every night until the wee hours of the morning. Every night after dinner he talked about the Bible, but I was long asleep or too young to remember what he was teaching. Reading the Bible at night must have been a family trait, or a Greek one, because my Uncle Andrew Kokas did the same thing every evening while enjoying his favorite brand of cigar.

SUMMERS IN POTTER VALLEY, CALIFORNIA

The second farm of my childhood was located in Potter Valley, California, about eighteen miles northeast of Ukiah. It was owned by Paul and Pearl Poulos, distant relatives of my dad.

I started going to the farm around the age of nine, spending summers and many holidays there. My parents were concerned initially that being around hay and the livestock would make my asthma flare up. Interestingly, while on the farm I never once had an asthma attack.

Paul and his brother Tom owned two restaurants in Ukiah. One of the reasons Paul raised pigs was that they could slop the pigs with food from the restaurants. The farm had a small dairy where we milked about fifty or so registered Holstein cows. There were also thirty or forty hogs and twenty to thirty sheep. The Poulos family kept the sheep because Pearl's brother, Uncle Bruce, was a professional herd dog trainer and used the herd to train dogs. The farm also had orchards and alfalfa fields.

Paul and Pearl had three sons. The oldest was from Pearl's first marriage and the other two, Paul Jr. and John, from her marriage to Paul. I never knew the oldest, but I quickly learned from John, who was closest to my age, that the topic of the oldest son wasn't one for discussion. All I ever learned was that he lived somewhere in the northern part of the state and was apparently very successful.

Paul Jr. and I got to know each other a little, but not for long. He was getting ready to go off to college at the University of California, Davis to fulfill his lifelong dream of becoming a veterinarian. He became a world-renowned veterinarian who specialized in animal cancer research. For a number of years, he worked and studied in Stockholm, Sweden, and Utrecht, The Netherlands, before returning to Ukiah and opening his own clinic.

John, the youngest, and I became great friends. He taught me a good deal about farming and animal husbandry, but most of all about responsibility and commitment. On the farm, as in life, there's no such thing as putting something off for tomorrow.

Years later, John went to college and finished his education at the University of California, Hastings College of the Law, where a plaque still hangs in his honor for having achieved the highest academic honors of any student. John graduated from law school first in his class and went on to marry the woman who finished number three. His field of expertise was water rights, an important subject for California farmers.

On the farm, I learned responsibility and commitment. If I agreed to do something it was an absolute, not a maybe. For example, the cows had to be milked twice a day and had to be fed. There were also about fifty acres of orchards and alfalfa that needed water. The local water district had communal watering. That meant you didn't know when you were going to get the water. Your turn could come at 2:00 a.m., and if it did, we got up and did whatever was needed to fill the rows with water. Rarely did Paul Sr. have to tell us to get out of bed and rarely did he have to remind us we had chores to take care of. In fact, the last thing we wanted was for him to remind us of a chore, since forgetting did not go over well with him.

Living on a farm is a life-altering experience, one I wish my sons could have had. Farm life helped me grow up to be a responsible adult and taught me respect and admiration for the farming profession.

Typically, our chores consisted of milking the cows twice a day, periodically irrigating the orchards and alfalfa fields, feeding the hogs, and cutting and baling hay. We also loaded the baled hay onto a tractor trailer and stacked it in the barn for the winter season.

I also learned how to strip a cow. Stripping a cow is getting the very last bit of milk out of it after the milking machine was removed from the cow's udder. One of our favorite games was to take an udder and squeeze it at the cats, who loved to catch the milk we tried to squirt into their mouths. It was great fun to watch the cats lick their faces when we missed. The challenge was to hit the cat square in the mouth, a much harder task than you might think.

Nothing like real-life exposure—on the farm, John and I learned about "the birds and the bees." During my farm years, I watched the breeding and delivery of many calves, pigs, and sheep. I also learned all about artificial insemination. That experience embedded in my mind that one day I would be present during the birth of my children. Back then, such a thing was unheard of, but I was there in the delivery room to witness the arrival of my three sons.

In case you're thinking that all we did were chores, we *were* kids and did get into mischief. I remember getting into trouble during irrigation chores. Irrigation was best done with two people, each holding a lantern. One of us would stand at each end of the watering ditch. We'd signal each other as the water started to enter the ditch and when the water reached the end of the ditch.

One day, we decided to see what chewing tobacco would be like, so we managed to get our hands on some. As we were walking up and down the rows during irrigation, we tried chewing the tobacco and got horribly sick from swallowing some of the tobacco juice. I think Pearl suspected what we'd done, but we never let on why we couldn't eat breakfast the next morning.

A Building Block Of Experiences

Nothing in life happens by accident. Everything and everyone we encounter affects us, although the effect may not be immediate. I recognize there will be those who don't agree that everything happens for a reason, but my whole life has been a building block of experiences, positive and negative.

Another time we tried smoking a cigar. Since we could only get our hands on one cigar, we passed it to each other walking the rows. I think back on those memories with a smile.

One week during the summer, John's first cousin (a girl) came to visit. John was quite an instigator, so as soon as chores were done, John suggested his cousin and I play strip poker. That sounded exciting, so I agreed. Before we started, I went up to my bedroom and put on more clothes under my overalls. I thought I was being a very smart kid. As the game progressed, I was losing so badly I was down to my bathing suit, so I decided to bail before it got too embarrassing. Of course, at that moment Pearl drove into the farm. We all ran to our respective rooms as fast as our feet could carry us, except for John, who stayed in the living room reading a book.

The Olympic Club

Before moving to Ukiah, Paul lived in San Francisco, where he and my dad were the first members of Greek descent to belong to The Olympic Club. In those years, the club was made up primarily of Irish and Italian members. During that time, women, African Americans, and Asians weren't allowed membership. Paul was an outstanding boxer in his youth, and Dad was an equally outstanding wrestler. I think The Olympic Club offered them both memberships because of their athletic prowess. Being a member of The Olympic Club was prestigious and required members to pay membership dues. Given that Paul and Dad were new immigrants and participated in Olympic Club sporting programs, they didn't have to pay the monthly dues. They were both given what we would call "scholarships." Over the years, my father sponsored many young men to become members of The Olympic Club. Dad was cautious about his behavior at all times when he was in the club, something he felt helped him become well-liked and accepted by other club members.

Pearl came in and asked where everyone was. John gave an answer but being the wise woman she was (and a schoolteacher), she could tell something was fishy.

Some days later, Paul Sr. pulled John and me aside and said he wanted to talk to us about men and the two heads they have. We both looked at him with quizzical expressions because we didn't know what two heads he was talking about.

He explained: "Every man has two heads: one on his shoulders and one in his pants." He went on to remind us to never let the one in our pants control the one on our shoulders. We definitely got the message. I've wondered if Pearl figured out what we had been up to and told Paul.

Being around farm animals, it was easy to get attached to them. One summer I became attached to a baby lamb. Every time I would get in the pen, it would run up and follow me around, so I began petting it and it quickly became a pet. Uncle Bruce warned me that farm animals weren't pets and to act like they were wasn't good for me or the animal. When butchering time came, Uncle Bruce asked me to help with butchering the lambs, and yes, one was my pet lamb. This meant killing, gutting, and skinning it. I stood there holding the lamb while the deed was done. That was the second time my heart was broken over a pet, but I learned if you live on a farm, getting attached to a farm animal is something you don't do.

One final lesson to share dealt with the use of artificial insemination on cows. One evening, over dinner, Paul Sr. explained that old Doc Muckchesnie Mortin would come by the next day to carry out the process of breeding the cows. Pearl loved to tell the story of my reaction. She would explain my eyes got very wide and my jaw dropped. She said you could see the wheel in my brain spinning.

I said, "I have to see this."

When Doc arrived, I was the first in the barn.

After his graduation and marriage, John returned to the farm, where he took over the house. By that time, I was married to my wife, Litsa and we went back to the farm to spend a weekend. That was the last time I saw John and his wife. I learned years later the two had separated. I must admit losing touch with John left a hole in my life. Sadly, after a brief email exchange with Paul Jr., I didn't keep in touch with Paul Jr., Paul Sr., or Pearl. I often think back on those years and feel guilty I made no real attempt to reconnect with people who played such an important role in my developmental years.

CHAPTER 6

Finding My Confidence

"You must give a full measure of yourself; if not, it's like
stealing from your employer or cheating yourself."
NICHOLAS J. PREOVOLOS, MY DAD

W HEN I WAS fourteen, I joined the California Chapter of the International Order of DeMolay. DeMolay is a "youth-led adult-advised" leadership organization dedicated to making young men better people and leaders. Alumni members include John Wayne, Pete Rose, Walt Disney, Dan Rather, Willard Scott, Burl Ives, and countless others. Leo Kumeloswa was a friend of my dad's and a member of the Masons and Shriners who suggested I join the Order of DeMolay, with him as my sponsor.

DeMolay had several precepts, each giving you a moral and ethical lesson. While other kids in my age group participated in school activities, I focused on DeMolay, which fulfilled my need to be active and creative.

Our chapter advisor was a man we called Doc Mosby. He was a high school teacher and a football coach. Doc Mosby was honored by the Masonic Order with the highest degree one could receive, that of a thirty-third degree of the Scottish Rite. He was an incredible man, and we were fortunate in many ways that he was our senior advisor. He was a wonderful human being, filled with kindness and love for children. Doc's wife's family belonged to the Daughters of the American Revolution. They were both extraordinary educators but had, to my knowledge, no children of their own. Doc passed away in the late 1960s, and he remains in my nightly prayers.

RAISING MONEY TO HELP OTHER KIDS

In our DeMolay chapter, I created a program to raise money for high school kids with cerebral palsy and to help send kids to camp. I had the idea of putting on a variety show and selling tickets to raise money. We called the show "Around the World with Sadie Hawkins." It featured songs and dances from around the world, including Greece, Germany, the Philippines, and Mexico. The program became an annual event.

To sell tickets, we created separate contests between the Rainbow Girls and the Job's Daughters, organizations that were the female counterparts to DeMolay. (All the organizations came under the supervision of the Masonic Order and Eastern Star organizations.) The girls would sell tickets, and the girl in each organization who sold the most tickets would be crowned queen.

Part of my responsibility was bringing the girls and the guys together to hire a professional folk dance instructor who could teach us various folk dances. One year, the teacher we hired quit about three weeks into the instruction. I don't think he was used to working with noisy, and at times, unruly teenagers. We still managed to pull it together and put on the show.

For our performances, we used one of the local high school's auditorium, thanks to Doc Mosby and his wife. The school allowed us to put on three performances during the weekend without charging us for using the space. Our only expense was paying for the stage crews, marketing, and programs.

The program proved successful, and for several years our performances helped send kids of high school age to a summer camp for a week or two. The first year, we raised enough money to send two kids, and the last year I was involved with the program we sent as many as eight kids to camp for two weeks.

HARD FACTS OF FUNDRAISING

DeMolay taught us lessons, including one that has stayed with me all my life. We wanted to donate the money we had raised to a local charity dealing with teenage disorders, but the charity initially elected to refuse it. The reason we were given was that the charity was part of the United Way. Had they taken the money, it would affect their budget and cause United Way to cut back on their allocation.

This made no sense to a bunch of teenagers, so we went to United Way headquarters in San Francisco to plead our case. After this experience, I took a closer look at the United Way's policies and realized if they were involved, we were required to give the money to them instead. In turn, they would parse it out to the organizations under their control, using some formula. We searched for a charity that was not tied to the United Way. We found one that would take our money and also sponsored programs for teenage kids and camping.

That United Way experience stayed with me. Years later, when I was employed by Wells Fargo, the major companies in the San Francisco area pushed for their employees to join the United Way fundraising campaign. It was an annual event, with executive leadership, pledge cards, and a televised in-office pitch. I never donated but would support the discussion with my staff.

On more than one occasion, Human Resources tried to convince me that I needed to be more cooperative or supportive of the program. I explained my position to no avail, until I noticed on a list of United Way charities that funds were going to Catholic and Jewish charities, but not Greek Orthodox charities. Confronted by HR the next year, I said I couldn't give because my favorite charity wasn't on their list.

BECOMING A POSSIBILITY THINKER

It seemed all the service clubs like DeMolay were trying to figure out how to make money. One day I raised my hand during a meeting and suggested having a dance and selling tickets. I was keen on holding the dance in one of the hotels with big, beautiful ballrooms. I was fourteen years old at the time.

After a lengthy discussion by the members, the Master Councilor invited me to make a motion to that effect. Parliamentary procedure was one of the things I would learn about in DeMolay as I went through the chairs (positions). I made a motion; it passed, and the Master Councilor appointed me chairperson for the event.

At the end of every chapter meeting, we had refreshments and played in a room with pool tables located in the Masonic Building where we met.

During that evening's social time, I immediately went up to Doc Mosby and said, "Doc, I am only fourteen. I can't do this." He assured me I could.

Doc Mosby asked if I had a Sunday suit, and I said "Yes." He told me to put on my Sunday suit and go to the hotel where I wanted the dance to be held. He said to tell them what I wanted, and they would introduce me to the people who handled those types of events.

I told him no one would pay attention to a fourteen-year-old, but he encouraged me. A few days later, I put on my best suit and went to the Fairmont Hotel.

The Fairmont is on top of Nob Hill, overlooking the city of San Francisco. I clearly remember walking up to the receptionist and telling her I represented the California Chapter of DeMolay, and we wanted to rent a ballroom for a dance.

While I was saying all of this, there was a gentleman standing behind her. She asked me to wait while she found someone to help me. I sat down and a few minutes later the receptionist returned. She then ushered me into a huge office filled with a lot of photographs and memorabilia.

Behind the big desk was the man who had been in the reception area. He asked me a few questions, and I explained who I represented and what we were trying to accomplish. He told me he was familiar with DeMolay, and it was clear he understood the fundraising project I had suggested. I told him we wanted to put on a formal dance for DeMolay boys, Job's Daughters, and Rainbow Girls.

He asked when we wanted to hold the dance, got out a calendar, and gave me the available dates. I told him I'd have to return to the chapter to verify the best date. He gave me thirty days to verify, and he would confirm it. As I was leaving, I noticed the nameplate on his desk read Ben Swig, but the name didn't mean anything to me.

That night at dinner, Dad asked how it went. I described what I had done, and Dad said it must have been a great experience for me to know I could do something like that. He then asked me who I had met with at the Fairmont, and I told him.

"Swig," Dad said, and smiled. "That's really impressive, son."

He asked me if I knew what this man's responsibilities were, and I said I did not, but I thought he helped people rent facilities. Dad then told me how lucky I was because Benjamin Swig was the owner of the Fairmont Hotel. I felt

Benjamin Harrison Swig, born in 1893, was a San Francisco real estate developer who purchased the Fairmont Hotel in San Francisco in 1945.

like I was ten feet tall and just hit a home run in the World Series.

We held the dance and selected a queen of the Rainbow Girls and the Job's Daughters. The dance was a success, and I was at a stage in my life that I thought I could do anything I put my mind to. That makes all the difference to a kid. If only I had applied that "do anything" spirit to my studies. I was creative from a young age. I suspect the formal dance may have been what put me over the top of being a possibility thinker.

TOO CREATIVE FOR MY OWN GOOD

As a teenager, I organized a ski trip to Lake Tahoe, a DeMolay event I chaired for about three years. I contracted with an agency to bring a busload of kids to Lake Tahoe and make the hotel reservations and ski arrangements. I was also responsible for making sure there were plenty of refreshments on the bus—which you can imagine included all types of beverages.

One year, my mother listened in on one of my phone calls when I was assuring the person on the other end of the line that yes, there would be beer on the bus. Guess what? I got busted big-time by my mother for this, and for having a fake ID. She told me people would assume the alcohol came from Dad. Not surprisingly, I ended up missing out on that particular trip. I have to admit, though, those were fun times. It helped when the travel agency gave me twenty silver dollars each year for being the event leader.

I also had hobbies I really loved, like stamp collecting, which Grandma Mabel helped me start. I have been a collector ever since those days, but today my collection is more focused on coins from antiquity. Among them is a piece of silver dating from the time of Jesus. Some days I hold the coin, wondering if it could have been among Judas's thirty pieces of silver. History is another subject that fascinates me.

When I acquired the coin, I visited my parish priest and explained that I wanted to have the coin blessed in case it had been among those used to pay Judas. The priest blessed the coin and placed it on the altar, where it remained for 90 days.

I also loved art and was a terrific artist until junior high. Some drawings I submitted at school were selected to be posted in the main hallway. I was very proud of my work. Then one day the paintings were gone. When I asked for them back, I was told they had been

Inspiring Our Children

How you deal with young people can affect the rest of their lives. Parents and adults sometimes forget how much of an impression we make on the minds of our children and how important it is to be not only a mentor to them, but also an inspiration. Help your kids become possibility thinkers. That is certainly what Doc and my parents instilled in me. They made it clear the only limitations on what I could do or become were those I placed on myself.

thrown away. After that experience, I didn't draw again until I got into college, and never had the same passion for it.

Adults, be careful how you deal with the gift of a child. What you do may affect them the rest of their lives.

Although many things from my childhood have dropped away over the years, the one thing that hasn't is my belief in myself and the belief that I can do anything I set my mind on. Even when taking on projects where only fools would rush in, by some stroke of fate I've gotten through.

CHAPTER 7

College Days

"The greatest gift you will receive from college is use of the library."
NICHOLAS J. PREOVOLOS, MY DAD

GRADUATED FROM LOWELL High School in 1958. Unfortunately, my high school years were devoid of academic accomplishment. In fact, if you read my yearbook, you'll see me described as "Debonair, personality kid...took part in football, swimming, and wrestling." The yearbook also stated I was going to go to Menlo College in preparation to become a lawyer.

The reality is, I did go to Menlo and worked on the library staff to earn extra money. And I did try my hand at studying law years later, after I graduated from college and got married, but it wasn't for me. And, at the time, I was far from being the world's best student.

My time at Menlo was about as undistinguished as it was in high school. I was an average student, mostly Cs and some Ds. I never got turned on to education. But college was something I knew I had to do. After taking the entrance exam and SATs (I had mediocre scores), my results were nothing to excite the entrance board of most schools.

I was never a great test-taker; tests always used to psych me out. I think if somebody had given me an oral exam, I would have done extremely well. But sitting down and taking a written exam didn't fit my personality, since my strongest skill was verbal communication.

Due to my low scores, I was rejected by all the colleges I had applied to, including Menlo. That bothered me immensely and I was determined to at least get into one of the colleges that had rejected me. I decided to go to the admissions director at Menlo College for a personal conversation. Although Menlo was a junior college, it also had a four-year business school that was highly regarded. My mind wasn't thinking "business" or even four years of college; I was solely focused on getting in somewhere. Had I applied myself and had any brains at the time, I would have tried to get into the business school or at least prove myself worthy of working hard in the junior college side.

At that time, Menlo catered to affluent young people. Its prep school, which was attached to the college, was also connected to Stanford. A lot of students who graduated from Menlo in the top 5 to 10 percent of the class went on to Stanford.

After Menlo turned down my application, I made an appointment with the director of admissions to plead my case in person. After listening to my arguments, he admitted me with the caveat that I had to maintain a certain grade point average or be dismissed.

I managed to stay within the grade range and after graduation was accepted at the University of Arizona in Tucson. I remember my father calling a dear friend and customer, Mike Buscos, who apparently had some connections at the U of A to help get me in.

Menlo was a good experience for me in many ways. It gave me a chance to do better in school as well as the opportunity to be around students of immensely varied backgrounds. For example, one of my classmates was the eldest son of the then crown prince of Saudi Arabia.

Doris Day's nephew attended, as did the son of Abbott, of Abbott and Costello fame. I remember one day when Day's nephew got drunk and raced his Triumph up and down the football field. He dug in a pretty good rut in the field, such that the school was ready to kick him out. Doris Day came on campus and paid to have it all taken care of, and he managed to stay in school.

Not to be forgotten, too, were the infamous Barry Beal and Carlton Beal Jr. from Texas. The brothers loved to play polo, so one day a large horse trailer carrying their polo ponies arrived, along with trainers. This meant they could play polo at the exclusive Atherton Country Club.

During my first semester at Menlo, I tried out for spring football, and lasted about a month. After a particularly hard practice, I came into the locker room, bleeding and sore. I remember complaining to one of my teammates, asking why the coach was being so hard on everyone since this was just a scrimmage.

He said something I needed to hear, which was that he needed to make it to the first string because he wanted to become a professional football player. That resonated with me and made me realize football wasn't for me. I took off my equipment, threw everything in the locker, and never looked back. So ended my football career.

The truth is, I have always been somewhat of an independent loner. I didn't have a lot of friends while growing up, but the ones I did have were close and had a positive influence on my life, and I on theirs. Most of my friends came from DeMolay.

Menlo College had service clubs in those years versus fraternities. Their brand of service wasn't like DeMolay; in addition, the service clubs had hazing, which I wasn't keen on. In fact, one of their tricks was to take the pledges up to San Francisco and get them to climb on the giant cables of the Golden Gate Bridge. I thought you had to be crazy to do it and I refused. Needless to say, I didn't last long in the service club and that was okay with me.

A young man who used to date Frank Sinatra's daughter was on campus. He was an interesting personality, actually a genius, but unfortunately a genius in the wrong direction. He was so cunning that before his first semester, he applied for a job with the school's maintenance crew. This gave him the opportunity to make a copy of the master keys to the facilities on campus, allowing his access to the documents needed for him to ace every exam. His last semester the school finally got suspicious and set a trap for him, caught him, and kicked him out.

As my father would say to us during one of our family dinners, "*O klefts ke of Pseftis to proto hrono heriti*," which translates to "The thief and the liar are only successful in the first year."

It seems as though all these personalities had some unique quality about them. On the day the crown prince's son arrived on campus, this big flatbed truck also came on campus with his brand-new Ferrari. He had more than one wife, but because he was in the US, he was only allowed to bring his "number-one wife" and servants. His family bought him a home in Atherton so he wouldn't have to live on campus.

I lived on campus during my Menlo years. Every weekend I took the bus from Menlo to San Francisco since my dad wouldn't let me have a car. Because I was going steady with a young lady who was in San Francisco, taking the bus was worth it. Occasionally, she came down to see me because her dad let her drive the family car, and she'd take me to San Francisco.

Around this same time, I started to work with Dr. Theodore Carleton in Oakland, a psychiatrist specializing in self-hypnosis. I found Dr. Carleton through my brother, Ted, who was studying to be a dentist. Ted wanted to use self-hypnosis techniques on his patients who couldn't tolerate the fear and anxiety of being at the dentist's office. My brother even used the technique with his wife when she delivered each of their three sons.

Dr. Carleton taught me how to hypnotize myself to help resolve some of my childhood medical issues that resurfaced in college. While at Menlo, the eczema that had been such a problem when I was young returned. I actually broke out in all the same areas I had when I was a kid. This occurred when I sat for my first-semester finals.

In those days, I was what we would call "high-strung," nervous about a lot of things, and I got anxious or impatient. For example, if I was taking a trip from point A to point B, my anxiety would kick in about getting to my destination. If I was driving and someone cut me off, I'd become enraged and flip them off. I look back on those days and shudder at the potential consequences.

Dr. Carleton taught me how to deal with these anxieties. For example, he taught me that when I took the bus home every weekend, I should, in effect, hypnotize myself. I relaxed during the trip and when I reached a certain point on the trip I automatically woke up. This worked like a charm.

Another thing that bothered me was waiting to get my hair cut. In those years, you didn't make an appointment; you just showed up and waited your turn. The waiting drove me crazy. Again, the technique was to tell the barber that when it was my turn, to tap me on the left shoulder. Instead of waiting and getting anxious, I sat in the chair and hypnotized myself, and then woke up when the barber touched that shoulder.

After two years, I graduated from Menlo, but not with any exceptional honors. I went on to the University of Arizona, where I finished my undergraduate degree with a major in US history and a double minor in political science and economics.

One thing I learned during my college years was that I could do what I made up my mind to do. The challenge was making up my mind.

My one claim to fame at the University of Arizona was when I joined the square dance club and danced around the state of Arizona at various county fairs. I had a lot of fun with that. But because I was so far away from home and only back in San Francisco for a few weeks of the year, I started to get lonely. Fortunately, there was a Greek church in town, St. Demetrios, where I quickly met a lot of kids, and became active in the church. I even wound up being a Sunday school teacher. I sang in the choir and eventually headed up the Sunday school. I must admit, had it not been for the church and the Greek community, I would have been a lost soul. Many decades later, my middle son, Nicholas, was to experience the same thing when he went to school in Phoenix.

While at the U of A, I had all my requirements to graduate except for one: language arts. I didn't know how I was ever going to graduate because I wasn't sure I could pass the course.

One of my Greek friends who was an exchange student told me there was a provision in the school regulations that a student could take a proficiency exam in another language instead of taking a language course. He encouraged me to apply to take the exam in Greek to fulfill my language arts requirement.

I told him my Greek needed work, so he suggested I talk to Mrs. Busios from church; he was certain she would help me. Sure enough, she did, and after several months of studying with her I took the proficiency exam. I passed. By the way, the proctor for the university on Greek language was Mrs. Busios, which I did not know at the time.

When I was at Menlo and the University of Arizona, I didn't have much interest in academics. However, one of my U of A classmates told me about a school called the Thunderbird International School of Management located in Glendale, outside of Phoenix. The more I learned about Thunderbird, the more it intrigued me. My dad was still willing to pay for my tuition, so I applied and was accepted. However, I had to wait a semester to enter Thunderbird, so I took the time to enter a new program at the U of A to get a teaching credential.

The U of A program was experimenting in using a Socratic method, bringing all the teaching disciplines together into the classroom. The holistic environment was exciting. Every morning was spent as a student teacher for US history at one of the local high schools. In the afternoon, we were back in class.

I probably could have taught in political science or economics, but both turned me off since I felt they were taught out of context. If you're discussing political science but not including history and sociology at the same time, a student can't get the flavor about what was really happening. Both subjects bothered me from this perspective.

My feeling is that these subjects should be taught in a holistic manner, so I switched to history. Although the bulk of my studies were in US history, I took some European history as well.

I went through the teaching program with the plan of becoming a history teacher. One of my strongest memories was being in the program the day President Kennedy was assassinated. I was teaching that very day when the announcement about his death came over the loudspeaker. It was a sobering day, one I remember distinctly.

Sadly, my experience as a student teacher went from good to bad. The teacher I was working under made fun of me because I assigned extracurricular reading for the students, reading that went above and beyond the textbook. I also never gave true-false questions, as he did; my tests were always essays.

He made comments like, "The kids don't care." I thought it was up to us to teach them to care.

One day in the teachers' lounge he was kind of making fun of me, and I pointed out he was still giving the same true-and-false exams he gave thirty years ago, and the kids all knew it—and they also knew the answers. I told him he was lazy—a comment that didn't set well with him, as you can imagine.

I discovered many other teachers were of the same ilk, a fact that turned me off to teaching. Maybe they had become jaded over the years or maybe they were tired of what they did. Nevertheless, I finished the curriculum and chose not to obtain my teaching certificate. I decided this wasn't what I wanted to do with my life.

After the student teaching semester, I entered the Thunderbird International School of Management and finally caught on fire. Instead of my usual mediocre work, I was getting As and Bs. I think that's because Thunderbird was a different environment than most schools. Thunderbird treated every student as an adult.

We all had to live on campus, as did the entire faculty. Every Wednesday and Friday night we'd gather poolside for beer and conversation. Every room had a refrigerator stocked with lots of booze and it wasn't unusual for professors to knock on the door, day or night, come in, chat, and have a drink. In fact, it was expected.

For the first time ever, I wasn't treated as a child. At Thunderbird, there was a sense of responsibility—the feeling that "we trust you." There was also the sense that the professors saw you as an equal. Students were treated like adults who were there to learn about international commerce. Everyone was willing to sit down and talk to you—to share their knowledge. They were also willing to go out to dinner with you, which is something I frequently did with a number of my teachers. In fact, two of them were guests at my wedding. The faculty was primarily made up of people who also had practical experience in the field, not just academic types.

After graduation, I was theoretically prepared for real life and a career in international business since I had been required to become proficient in a second language. In terms of practicality, that meant I needed a second- or third-grade level of language proficiency and vocabulary. My choices at that time were French, Portuguese, Spanish, and German. My choice was Spanish.

My best friend at school was the Portuguese teacher, Senorita DeNaronia, who was an amazing woman. She came from Portuguese royalty. I believe her father was a general in the Portuguese army. She came to the US to escape the tyranny of World War II. Most of her family had been killed during the war, but amazingly she remained a fun-loving lady. She was tremendous.

After graduating from Thunderbird, I was offered a job at Continental Grain. The plan was to go to New York as a trainee and then work at their operation in northern Greece, outside of Thessaloniki. My dad's health was failing at the time due to emphysema, although he never smoked a day in his life and had been a lifelong athlete. Even with emphysema he could still swim ten laps every day at the indoor pool at The Olympic Club. His emphysema was a result of developing asthma in his fifties.

I told Dad about the opportunity in New York to work for Continental Grain, and he said, "Now that I got one foot in the grave, you are going to New York. When will I get to see you and enjoy you?" I asked him if he wanted me to come home. He did, so I went back to San Francisco.

Ironically, one of my roommates, a Texan named Jim Wright, accepted a job with Bank of America for $400 a month. He encouraged me to interview with them, but I told him $400 a month wasn't worth it. As it turned out, I ended up in San Francisco—like Jim—but without a job.

In terms of my career, Dad didn't care what field I went into, as long as I did the best job I could. I know a lot of parents put pressure on their kids to be one thing or another, but my parents never did. Instead, they emphasized giving 100 percent to whatever you chose to do.

I'll never forget one of my other classmates at the University of Arizona—a brilliant kid whose parents had both graduated from Stanford and were doctors working for Kaiser. In their minds, he was going to become a medical doctor, too. In our third year of college, he tried to commit suicide. The father came down to school while my classmate was still in the hospital.

The attending doctor said, "You know, your son feels that you are demanding too much from him." The conversation went on and the doctor revealed the son's interest was not in medicine, but he did not want to let his parents down.

The father sat down with his son after he got out of the hospital, and said, "What is it you want to do?"

He replied, "I want to be a cabinetmaker."

The father said, "Okay, let's find the best damn place to learn to be a cabinetmaker."

They found a place in Germany, where the kid went to study, and then he went on to become a multimillionaire making cabinets because of the explosion of housing in the US and the need for his type of work.

I admit it took a while for me to grow up, to become more mature, and I attribute Dad's wisdom and principles to my growth. He gave me a set of standards upon which to build a foundation. I have always said if I could be one-quarter as successful as my father, I would consider myself a success. Dad came to the US with a third-grade education, learned the language (and learned it well), and became an insatiable reader. In fact, Dad never stopped reading his entire life. On the day of his death, a book he had been reading fell to the floor.

Dad read everything from the newspaper and *Reader's Digest* to history and philosophy. He loved stories and books written about people he admired, such as Albert Schweitzer and Mahatma Gandhi. People who made a difference fascinated him. Growing up with Dad left a stamp on me; I've had an inner fire that aroused my passion to also make a difference in the world.

Dad was proud of his ancestral history and wanted us to understand who the Greeks were, as well as their contribution to the world's culture. I am always reminded of the movie, *My Big Fat Greek Wedding*, in which the father would say a word in English and claim its root came from Greek, which was true in some cases.

I remember Dad asking us, "Do you know how many Greek words are in the English language? There are 140,000 Greek words in the English language." He said that with pride, even knowing that the English language has tens of thousands of Latin, French, and German words. But 140,000 of them were Greek.

Dad's commitment to honesty and fairness was amazing. Never once did I see Dad express any form of discrimination toward anyone. I think a lot of that was based on his experiences as a young immigrant.

CHAPTER 8

First Jobs

"As long as the music is playing, you've got to get up and dance."
CHARLES PRINCE, FORMER CHAIRMAN AND CEO OF CITIGROUP

M Y FIRST REAL job was delivering newspapers every afternoon when I was nine years old. My job was to buy my papers, deliver them, and collect money from my customers every month. If I wanted to increase my route or the number of customers, I had to call on people in my route area to solicit a subscription. The responsibility of delivering those papers rain or shine taught me discipline. I also learned basic business concepts such as bookkeeping and balancing a checkbook.

The Tower Market, 1942. Photo by Jacqueline Proctor.

When I was a teenager, I worked as a box boy at the Tower Market at 635 Portola Drive (now Mollie Stone's Tower Market) in the Twin Peaks area of San Francisco.

I worked on weekends and holidays, and it was a job that required me to join the Retail Clerks union. It was a great learning experience, because I was exposed to direct customer contact in a neighborhood store whose customers included people of great wealth, along with those of a solid, middle-class background. I quickly discovered there are all kinds of people in this world.

I once bagged groceries for baseball player Willie Mays' first wife, a woman who came across to me as not very polite or generous, yet extremely demanding. I learned to shrug it off when I discovered that sometimes such behavior goes along with the territory of being married to a famous athlete.

My third job, before graduating from college and entering the real world, was working for Southern Pacific Railroad. Southern Pacific had a policy back in the fifties and sixties stating that the children and relatives of officers of the company could work at summer jobs during their college years. Perry Spackman, a family friend, helped me get a job there. Every summer during college, I worked for Southern Pacific as a passenger reservation clerk, with a salary of twenty-five dollars a day. At the time, that was considered good pay. As with all my jobs, this one taught me a valuable lesson: I didn't want to work for railroads.

All of us summer workers were situated in a passenger reservations room that contained a huge carousel six levels high, with each level representing a particular train and each cubicle in the level representing a car. In front was an iron bar you would grab to move the carousel around. All the clerks wore a phone headset and would receive calls from train agents to reserve a seat, room, or bedroom suite. We would turn to the correct level on the carousel, pull out the reservation booklet, write in the name of the passenger, and confirm the train and car number with the agent. Everything was done by hand, of course.

There was a huge blackboard with a quote from the president of the railroad, saying: "It costs us a quarter of a million dollars to build a passenger car; it only costs us $8,500 to build a freight car. Which do you think is the most profitable?" The message was clear. Southern

Pacific didn't really want passenger business; for them, the money was in freight.

The unfortunate part of this mindset was that Southern Pacific did not fully appreciate their own business; they merely saw themselves as freight forwarders, as opposed to being in the transportation industry. Because of this, the airline, shipping, and trucking industries quickly encroached on both their passenger and freight businesses. Had they thought of themselves as being in the transportation business, they might own the other transportation industries today. It's an example of how management can lead a company to success or failure.

After college, my dad encouraged me to get a real estate license. I took and passed the exam, and in 1965, I went to work for a fellow named Sal Cordova. Sal had a small real estate office, and his entire business model was buying houses for his own personal portfolio. A fine man, Sal was not a mentor or a teacher. Had he been, I probably would have had a career in real estate.

Shortly after I joined Sal, the US went through its first major credit crunch of the twentieth century and rates shot up to 7 percent, sending shockwaves through the economy and the real estate market. Any success I might have had quickly went out the door with the new interest crisis. But I believe the good Lord had other plans for me.

Sal had connections with the unions in Los Angeles, specifically with the International Brotherhood of Teamsters. The Teamsters called on Sal with specific instructions about acquiring real estate in different areas. One day Sal sent me to West Oakland to look at several old Victorian-style apartments. In those years, West Oakland was extremely economically depressed.

My job was to assess vacant apartments and appraise their condition. It was hard to believe what I found there. All of the old-style floor heaters had been stolen, the clothes hooks in the closets were gone, and the old-fashioned pulley ropes in the weighted windows had been cut—and that was just on the first floor.

In the middle of the kitchen floor was a steel plate measuring four feet by four feet and about a quarter-inch thick. This is where the tenants did their cooking because the gas and electric company had turned off the power, something they cannot legally do today. You can imagine what the kitchen looked like, blackened from the smoke.

As I went through the apartments, things only got worse. Because the water had been turned off, the tenants couldn't flush the toilets. By the time I got home that evening I felt so filthy and contaminated that as I reached the front door of our apartment, I took off all my clothes at the entrance.

My wife, Litsa, answered the door to find me undressing in the hall. Her look of shock made me wish I had a camera.

All I could say was, "Don't touch me until I can take a shower." I then put the clothes in the garbage chute across the hall, went into the apartment, and showered.

A few weeks later, Sal again asked me to go to West Oakland because the Teamsters were looking for property. This time the property was an apartment complex and an abandoned theater. I met the so-called manager, who took me around to inspect the building. I noticed none of the apartments had a traditional key, but instead each one had a padlock. The rent rolls indicated a 90 percent occupancy rate. I wanted to see some of the rooms, and they were all basically the same: a broken-down couch, a coffee table, a filthy reclining chair, and bedrooms with mattresses on the floor. I asked him if people rented the rooms by the hour because the place looked like a whorehouse. He assured me that was not the case. I took photos of the property and headed back to the office. Disenchanted with the world of real estate, I left the industry.

Next, I found a job with Del Monte, the canning giant known for The Cannery, a San Francisco landmark. In 1909, it was the largest fruit and vegetable cannery in the world, famous for its assortment of pickles and unique ketchup made with pineapple vinegar.

At Del Monte, I was assigned part of the San Francisco territory that included small grocery and mom-and-pop stores. Each sales rep was given a company car. Now I felt like I had a "real" job.

Every day, off we went, calling on customers. First stop was always the back of the store to what was called the "spoils bin." Each supplier had their own bin where dented cans and broken bottles of your product were stored. We would add up the cost of the spoiled goods and write a check, on the spot, for their value. We had to hand over a check before the buyer would even discuss any promotional offers, let alone give us a new order.

Del Monte didn't want the spoils back, so I took the cans that were just dented. My mother loved this; we had cans of tuna and dried fruit sitting in our garage. It was many years after I left Del Monte before they were all consumed.

The job had a lot of structure that was unfamiliar, which gave me a new understanding of workplace discipline. We had weekly sales meetings to prepare us for our time in the field, as well as to introduce us to new products, new promotional deals, and better sales techniques. The meetings were also supposed to get the sales force pumped up to work harder. This type of "inspiration" was never a good fit with me, emotionally or intellectually. I was also immature and perhaps naïve about what was expected of me.

There was another part of the job that troubled me. It entailed carrying a satchel that held two porcelain trays, a can opener, and a spatula. We would go into a store and say: "I will cut against anybody's product to prove that our product is better." We would buy a competitor's can of green beans, open it, and dump it onto one of the trays, and then dump the green beans from a Del Monte can onto the other tray. We'd demonstrate our product's superiority using the spatula to "cut" the vegetables, to point out the difference in quality between our product and that of our competitor. The problem was you couldn't really see a difference between the two products.

At one of our sales meetings, I said I wasn't doing any cutting anymore. My boss asked which products I was cutting against. Libby's and S&W, I said, but even with the off-brands like Mission Pak green beans, we were having a hard time. Cutting made us look bad and we were wasting the buyers' time.

The sales director explained we were having difficulties because as seasonal produce began to run out, companies would call on their competitors to ask if they were running a surplus. It was common practice in the food and beverage industries at the time for competitors to relabel each other's products and sell them under their own brand name.

Another salesman spoke up to confirm he was having the same trouble, to no avail. All in all, my canned sales career was going nowhere. My performance results slid, and I was eventually released from the company.

CHAPTER 9

Career Development

"The impossible is often the untried."
JAMES "JIM" GOODWIN, IRISH FOOTBALL COACH AND FORMER PLAYER

AFTER MY BRIEF stint in real estate and my time at Del Monte, I looked for a job in the international field, using what I had learned from graduate school in the field of international commerce. I was also attending law school at night.

I landed an interview at Wells Fargo Bank. The interviewer asked if I had ever considered a career in trust services. That one question set the path for my future. I was finding I lacked the patience and commitment to study law. The Trust Department was something I saw as the path to a career, although I knew nothing about trust services.

After the Wells Fargo recruiter talked to me about all the benefits and the bank's junior management training program, he

Photo sent to me by Lee Ruggles of McCann Erickson, Inc. advertising agency in San Francisco, June 14, 1971

had my attention. The offer was for a salary of $580 per month. At the time, my wife was making a little more than that as a teacher in Daly City, California, outside of San Francisco.

As I reflect back on those days, we didn't have much and didn't need much, but we lived a very good life. We learned to fly an airplane, got our pilot's licenses, traveled, and enjoyed life. In October 1969 we bought our first home. On January 13, 1970, our first son, Athanasios "Thanasi" Constantino was born. On August 15 of that year, my name day, my father passed away.

SETTLING INTO LOS ANGELES

By 1970, I had received two promotions, advancing from trust administrator to assistant trust officer to trust officer. My assignment was to open trust operations and investment counseling facilities, which then became my responsibility. Wells Fargo was expanding into Southern

Wells Fargo Bank branch, Century City, California, color print, circa 1967. Copyright ©1999-2021 Wells Fargo Bank, N.A.

California and they wanted to open a trust office in Los Angeles. I was invited to consider becoming an assistant vice president in charge of pension and investment counseling services for all of Southern California. Litsa and I were looking for a change, so I accepted the promotion.

As I reflect on this time, there were some challenges within the larger family environment that influenced our development as a couple. I was perhaps still immature, not yet ready to step up to the plate and be 100 percent committed to establishing our unique "kingdom" as both of our parents had done. Maybe putting space between us and the larger family would allow us to devote our attention to each other and continue to lay the foundation of a strong marriage.

We left San Francisco after Thanasi was born. We sold our house within three months and were fortunate to locate a temporary home at the Park La Brea apartment complex in Los Angeles. Everything was falling into place, which confirmed the decision we had made was absolutely the right thing for us.

I must admit that in spite of my good fortune and great job, I was still immature and full of myself. Struggling to find out who I was and trying to figure out what I was going to do with the rest of my life, it was slowly dawning on me that I was the only person who could determine my future. I had my first child, after all. It was a sobering experience that forced me to get more serious about the work I was doing and where it might lead. There is nothing like increasing responsibility to help push you along in your development and career prospects. I had dreams of owning my own business, but I didn't quite have the courage to venture out of the protective arms of Wells Fargo.

For San Franciscans, especially those born and raised in the city, it's heresy to even think of leaving for Los Angeles. But I did. I think LA is an exciting town and whatever Northern California thinks they have, LA has ten times of it. The problem is, it's spread out for miles and didn't seem to have the appearance of being a very sophisticated city, but it was.

Around the time we moved to LA, the city's cultural scene was expanding. The Performing Arts Center of Los Angeles County for music, opera, and more had just opened downtown. Building the center was courageous; at that time, downtown LA had deteriorated to little more than a slum. The center was a true infusion of hope for downtown LA.

By late 1970, we began to take living in LA seriously, thinking it was going to be our permanent home. In 1972, our second son Nick was born at Cedars-Sinai Medical Center in LA and baptized at Annunciation Cathedral in San Francisco. Spiro was born two years later and baptized at the Saint Sophia Greek Orthodox Cathedral, built by Charles Skouras of Twentieth Century Fox fame. Because we had little kids and no relatives to step in and babysit, we didn't have a lot of mobility and our involvement with the church in LA was limited to going to church on Sundays and holy days.

To get better acquainted with the area, I reactivated my real estate license and found a realtor who was willing to let me hang my license in his office. This gave me the opportunity to look at properties and try my hand at getting listings.

One day, the realtor I was working for on weekends found a piece of property in Glendale, a beautiful suburb of Los Angeles, often called a bedroom community. The property, a house built in the early 1900s, had not been cared for in years. It sat on a lot measuring 100' x 200'. The realtor introduced me to a builder who wanted to partner with someone to buy the property and split the lot. His goal was to build a home for his daughter, who had a child the same age as our Thanasi. We partnered with him, built our own home, and lived in it until 1974, when another unexpected opportunity came knocking at our door. In fact, there were two incredible opportunities.

NEW OPPORTUNITY IN SAN DIEGO

At work, I was trying to put the Wells Fargo Trust Department on the map. Up until 1968, Wells Fargo had no branches south of Bakersfield. Security Pacific National Bank, the second-largest bank in California, had no branches farther north than Bakersfield. The two banks had aspirations of merging, but there was an issue with an old-line Jewish family, the Ehrmans, who owned a significant interest in both banks. Their name also appeared on a prominent law firm headquartered in San Francisco, Heller Ehrman LLP. After 118 years in business, Heller's partners voted to dissolve the firm on September 26, 2008, in the wake of its lender bank's decision to freeze the firm's accounts.

When Wells Fargo and Security Pacific announced they were planning to merge, the Justice Department approved, on the condition that the Ehrmans relinquished their control. The merger would have given the family a powerful 36 percent controlling interest of a major bank. The family refused and the merger didn't go through. (Both

Wells Fargo and Security Pacific Bank went on to develop statewide banking operations.)

In 1974, Wells Fargo offered me a promotion to return to San Francisco and head up the National Investment Marketing Services, which I accepted. However, things were held up for a few months due to another acquisition by Wells Fargo in Los Angeles, this time of Beverly Hills National Bank. During that time, Southern California First National Bank (SCFNB) offered me a position in San Diego.

I was initially interviewed by F. Seth Brown, who was the head of the Trust Department at SCFNB. Brown was a member of the upper crust of the San Diego/La Jolla community and served as commodore of the San Diego Yacht Club. Richard T. "Dick" Silberman, bank president, interviewed me next.

During the interview, Silberman periodically asked me what I wanted to achieve in the way of status, position, and compensation. He returned to that question of *what else?* several times during the interview. I originally had no intention of accepting the offer, but when I ran out of "what else" answers, it dawned on me at that moment that I had accepted the position, and we were on our way to San Diego.

(An engaging and bright individual, Silberman's interview style was so impressive, I went on to use the same technique when interviewing prospective employees.)

Another factor in my decision was that as much as I loved Wells Fargo, the new position in San Francisco would have required extensive travel and time away from home.

WELLS FARGO EXIT INTERVIEW

At the time, Wells Fargo allowed officers with the title of assistant vice president or above to choose any of the bank's top four officers for their exit interview. Bank President Richard P. "Dick" Cooley was my first choice, but he was on his way to Japan for the opening of Wells Fargo's first branch there. Ernest C. "Ernie" Arbuckle, chairman of the board, conducted my exit interview.

The day of the meeting, I went up to the executive offices of the bank on Montgomery Street in San Francisco. You can imagine they were beautifully appointed. I was ushered into Ernie's office. He invited me to sit on the couch while he sat on a chair directly across from me.

He said, "Peter, Peter. What have we done to you that you want to leave us?"

"Nothing," I replied. "But may I share a dream I keep having?"

In the dream, I was at my retirement party. Ernie handed me a gold watch and I looked at it, thinking, "Is that all there is for devoting thirty-five years of my life to the company?"

He laughed heartily. He then questioned me regarding what I knew about the bank I was going to work for. I was aware of its excessive loan loss reserve position and other challenges it faced. It seemed like an opportunity for me to demonstrate my potential to be a problem solver. He agreed and expressed pleasure that I had done my homework.

When I left, he extended his hand and wished me well.

"If you ever want to come back, please give me a call and you will have your job back," he said.

That comment made me feel so great and so important that I was ready to conquer anything. It took me back to that fourteen-year-old boy who met with Ben Swig of the Fairmont Hotel.

SAN DIEGO'S COMPLICATED WORLD OF BANKING

Describing the process leading up to my accepting the position in San Diego involves some name-dropping. It was also a learning experience for me.

SCFNB had been taken over by Robert O. "Bob" Peterson and Richard T. "Dick" Silberman in 1967. Peterson, a San Diego businessman and entrepreneur, opened the first Jack In The Box restaurant at 6270 El Cajon Boulevard in San Diego. Peterson and his company, which became Foodmaker, Inc., got involved with Silberman during this time. In 1968, Peterson sold Foodmaker to Ralston Purina Co.

Peterson went from hamburgers to banking and philanthropy. He and Silberman took over SCFNB by acquiring only 13 percent of the outstanding stock. Within a short time, the bank appeared to operate as if it were a piggy bank for a few leaders. Eventually, the trouble led to a huge loss reserves position mandated by bank regulations. That was about when I joined them. I was fully aware the bank was having trouble but didn't realize how much.

The bank started to have lending problems in the late 1960s. About five years before I was hired as head of the Employee Benefit Trust Department, it had $100 million in assets, but that had dwindled to $20 million. Most of the assets had bled off to a competitor, San Diego Trust & Savings Bank. The division of the Trust Department I took over was Pension Services. My job was to restore, stabilize, and build up that department.

The four years and eleven months that I was there, I helped rebuild the department, adding $200 million in new assets. In return, I received one raise during that time, and ended up getting fired.

My immediate supervisor was Seth Brown, who was a nice man but someone I considered a poor manager and leader. Seth hired bright, talented individuals. Unfortunately, the moment the well-qualified people he'd brought into the bank began to demonstrate their abilities, he would undermine their efforts. It seemed to me that he perceived them as threats.

INITIATING AN INCENTIVE PROGRAM

I wanted to hire my own salespeople and incentivize them by paying a commission. I found an incredible salesman named Charles "Chuck" Wert, who had worked with Security Pacific in the Audit Department and later joined California First Bank in its Trust Department in Orange County. He approached me about working in the pension area at SCFNB and I submitted his resume to HR. They hesitated to transfer him because of his lack of experience in the pension field. For me, his lack of knowledge about pensions was a plus because I knew I could teach him what he needed to know. I wanted someone who was smart, a hard worker, and a quick learner. Chuck had all those characteristics. I knew from the first time I met him that he was going to be a winner. I finally convinced HR to hire him. They put him on the low end of the pay scale. I assured him I would do everything I could to improve his situation.

The next step was to convince Seth Brown that we needed to create an incentive program for all our trust sales personnel. Donald A. Levi, the head of Trust Marketing and Sales, was an advocate of the concept who convinced Seth to approve the program. Don was one of those extraordinary team players and a hard worker; he also was a member of a prominent San Diego family of businesspeople and philanthropists, dating back to the 1860s. I'm not sure I fully appreciated him in the early days. He was an outstanding, ethical individual and most savvy.

Once the incentive pay program was put in place, Chuck went into high gear. After two years, he had become an incredible salesperson, far better than I could have imagined and far better than I was at selling. He was the only salesman besides Don Levi in the Trust Department who ever made a commission, to my recollection. I found that fascinating.

Every quarter that commissions were paid, I had to sign off on Chuck's commission voucher. About the third time I signed off, Seth came into my office and said if Chuck kept this up, he would be making more money than I was. Chuck's base-pay then was $18,000 and mine was $25,000. My response was that it was great, because if he did, it would mean the program was working as intended. Seth just never got the idea.

Chuck not only caught up, but he also surpassed me. Seth never stopped reminding me that Chuck was making more money than me. I once told Seth it seemed to bother him far more than it did me. I also added that I should get a raise because I supervised Chuck. As you can imagine, that went over like a lead balloon.

During one quarter, Seth told me that with his commissions, Chuck was on target to make twice as much as I was. Seth felt Chuck should only have made half of what he was earning. I said he deserved every dollar because he was creating an ongoing revenue stream; that year Chuck was adding a recurring revenue stream of $150,000 to my department. I began to realize that at the pace Chuck was going, he could pass Seth in compensation, and Seth wouldn't be able to handle that emotionally, in spite of his significant personal wealth. I warned Chuck that the day I left would be the day Seth closed down the incentive program.

A COSTLY ACCOUNTING ERROR

In 1975, a suspicious accounting error in the bank's retirement plan was discovered, involving the allocation of company stock. Several of the executives appeared to have been shorted in the number of shares they should have been credited with. At the time, our shares were selling for seven dollars per share, but when the Bank of Tokyo acquired the bank, the purchase price increased to eighteen dollars per share, a huge difference. The error didn't originate in my department because we had nothing to do with the plan recordkeeping. That was done internally by the Operations Department, supposedly because of the sensitive nature of the information involved.

I was asked, after my analysis, to report to Chairman of the Board Alden W. Johnson. In the meeting were two senior officers from the Bank of Tokyo. I described and explained what I knew the problem was and was candid about my findings, suggesting there was more to this problem than met the eye. I stated our investigation found one of the fund managers had made an innocent mistake that was easily correctable, but Operations' mistake compounded the problem.

Changing Banks

A little history on the evolution of Southern California First National Bank (SCFNB): By the seventies, SCFNB had become First National Bank. First National later became California First Bank, following its purchase by the Bank of Tokyo of California in 1975. Today, it's part of Union Bank.

Shortly after the meeting, I was called into Seth's office, and he advised me to fire John, an accounting clerk in my department, because of the error. I told him John had nothing to do with it; one of the women in my department who handled the account had made one of the key mistakes and I recommended she be put on probation, not fired. His response was that we were not going to fire the female in my department, but someone had to be the scapegoat. That was so repugnant to me that I was determined to do something about it.

A few days later, I invited John into my office and asked him to sit away from the door. I then called Seth and asked him if he could come to my office because I wanted to show him something of importance. As Seth crossed the threshold, I turned to John and told him that Seth had something very important to tell him, namely that his employment was ending. I knew once I did this, my days were numbered at the bank, but I no longer cared.

I had started to build my own company, Alpha & Omega Financial Management Consultants, Inc., while still working at the bank. We incorporated in 1975 with my wife, Litsa, serving as president. I had to be careful not to create the appearance of a conflict of interest. Alpha & Omega developed business that did not compete with the bank and its services. At that time, we were specializing in managing the financial affairs of high-net-worth individuals, like entertainers and athletes.

In late April 1979, Seth asked me to leave. He told me one day I'd thank him for this. So, I will do that now: Thank you, Seth. You gave me the courage to build my own business. I'm just sorry he isn't alive to read this.

CHAPTER 10

New Beginning: Alpha And Omega

"I learned to always take on things I'd never done before. Growth and comfort do not coexist."
VIRGINIA ROMETTY, CEO OF IBM

E VER SINCE I graduated from college, I had foreseen or at least dreamed of owning my own business; I just didn't know what it would be or how to go about it. Now I was able to fully commit myself to the endeavor we called Alpha and Omega.

At the time, my wife and I had three little boys, a car payment, a home mortgage, and $5,000 in the bank. Not much for someone without a job trying to start a business.

I immediately put together a business plan and budget. I started to market my plan, asking if any of my banking connections would lend us $50,000, which is what I thought it would take to get us started.

Lowell Halleck, president of the Bank of San Diego, was someone I knew from his days at San Diego Trust and Savings Bank. He was willing to lend me the money. I had to give him a second deed of trust on my home. From that initial capital, we paid our bills, produced a brochure, and started calling on potential clients.

Jimmy the Greek Snyder became our first client, thanks to an airplane flight, our shared Greek heritage, and my ability to show him how we could oversee some of his business affairs. Jimmy the Greek was a sport commentator who became well known for appearing on the CBS network's show, *The NFL Today*. We ended up providing total business management services to Jimmy, including supervising aspects of his business transactions, managing his gambling activities, and overseeing various contracts, including his contract with CBS.

I met Jimmy on a flight from Los Angeles to San Diego on a Friday afternoon. Jimmy was coming to San Diego to speak at a certified public accountants annual conference. I was still working for California First

Alpha & Omega's first client, Jimmy "the Greek" Snyder (left) with Governor Paul Laxalt of Nevada.

Bank, commuting between San Diego, Los Angeles, and San Francisco as part of a management team working with the Bank of Tokyo.

On the plane, the associate who was with me took the window seat and I took the middle seat. Someone sat in the aisle seat and then quickly got up and moved farther back. Shortly thereafter, a second person came and sat in the seat.

As the plane started taxiing, my associate told me to look under the legs of the individual sitting next to me. I did and turned back to her.

"Gosh, a suede attaché case," I said.

She told me to look at the gold lettering on the briefcase. In gold letters it read: JIMMY THE GREEK SNYDER. I turned and looked up to him (Jimmy was a big man, around six foot four) and spoke to him in Greek.

"Are you Greek?"

He answered, "Yeah, kid. Are you Greek?"

"Yes, sir."

By this time, the flight attendants were coming around and Jimmy wanted to treat my companion and me to a drink. We agreed. He wanted to know what I did for a living, and I explained I was in the pension field, designing retirement plans for individuals and corporations.

"Is that legal?" he asked.

I responded by saying it was absolutely legal. He got mad, and as only Jimmy could, used some four-letter words to express his disgust. He went on to tell me how much he spends on attorneys and CPAs, and how none of them had ever suggested he could set up a defined benefit pension plan.

By now, the flight attendants were coming around to collect for the drinks, and in typical Greek fashion, we began to argue about who was going to pay. I reached into my pocket and pulled out my puny money clip that at best may have had fifty dollars in it. He pulled out his bankroll—and I am not exaggerating—it was at least three inches thick, with a rubber band around it.

I held my money clip up against his fist of rolled-up money and said, "Yours is much bigger than mine, so you get to buy."

He laughed and said, "I like you, kid."

Jimmy wanted to know more about what I did and how it worked. I told him if he provided the information I needed, I'd do a study he could take to his attorneys and accountants. If they couldn't shoot a hole in it, Jimmy would pay my bill. I told him if he didn't like what I proposed, he wouldn't owe me anything. He pushed to know what it was going to cost him, but I repeated that if he liked the plan, he'd pay the bill, and if not, he'd owe nothing. Jimmy finally agreed, probably because my proposition appealed to his gambler's instincts.

He eventually said, "That's a deal, kid. Here's my business card." On the back he wrote the name of his accountant and told me to contact him for whatever I needed.

After a few days, I got a call from Jimmy's CPA, who sent me all the information I needed. I asked John Stoller, a good friend in San Francisco who owned his own third-party administrator (TPA) firm, to run the numbers for me. John taught me most of what I know about the pension fund business. He was a great mentor and a class act.

I called Jimmy and told him I wanted to present my ideas to him. I flew to Las Vegas and met his wife, Joan; their three children, Jamie,

Stephanie, and Anthony; and of course, their French poodle, Napoleon. We met in his home office and went through the various options. He settled on a defined benefit plan, and after my presentation he started to interview me as if I was applying for a job. He stated he was looking for someone he could trust to look after his affairs, and in general, be his manager.

He followed that by saying, "Can you manage someone like me?"

"Why, of course," I said.

I had never managed anyone up to this point in my career.

The conversation continued for well over an hour. As it was coming to an end, he asked me a question.

"How much larceny do you have in you?"

My mind was racing with what to say. I thought if I said none, he would know I was lying. Finally, I said I wasn't sure, but maybe 10 percent.

He said "Okay, you're hired."

I was so excited I could hardly wait to get back home and tell my wife all about it.

"You've never managed anybody before," was Litsa's reply.

We'd have to learn on the job. As is often the case, she was worried sick that we'd screw something up. Of course, we both were worried about how we'd do this without causing a problem at the bank. That was when we decided we needed to incorporate, and my wife would become the president.

So, Jimmy became Alpha & Omega's first client. He was initially paying us $800 per month plus out-of-pocket expenses. From that day forward, we have never looked back. God has blessed us and obviously His hand has guided us through the years.

Our work for Jimmy included analyzing his contracts and his payroll and preparing his tax returns. I managed his excess funds and designed and administered his pension plan.

I left the bank in 1979, right around the time CBS wanted Jimmy to join *CBS Sports* as an oddsmaker on the weekly NFL games, as well as a professional gambler and skilled marketing genius. He founded the

Worldwide Poker Tournament in Las Vegas and negotiated to bring Wayne Newton to "Sin City."

Jimmy's first contract with CBS that Alpha & Omega helped negotiate was for a quarter of a million dollars a year. Of course, it contained some unique clauses that dealt with gambling and behavior that might embarrass CBS. The president of *CBS Sports* at the time was a personal friend of his and Jimmy knew how much his friend was risking in hiring him. He never did anything to void the contract or embarrass his friend.

I reminded him that he had to be cautious about gambling. One of the biggest risk factors with him was that it is illegal to have side bets at the horse track, which was his favorite gambling hobby. He bet on the horses (which was legal), but also placed side bets with his cronies, such as which horse was going to come in last, which one was going to finish in the middle of the pack, etc. They played all kinds of crazy combinations. Unless you knew the codes, when you looked at the racing form on the side margins it merely looked like scribbles. Jimmy and his friends understood what they meant. They never exchanged money at the track. They always settled up after, away from the track, and many times not the same day or in the same city.

In all the years I worked with Jimmy, I only gambled once, when I went to the Kentucky Derby with him. I bet two dollars on a horse to show, and I think I won six dollars. I was so eager to go and collect my winnings that I made Jimmy late to our dinner meeting. He was understandably upset; Jimmy hated to be late. Besides, an average bet for him was easily one hundred dollars or more; my two-dollar bet making him late infuriated him.

"I could have given you the six dollars," he said. Of course, that would not have given me the same thrill.

Working and traveling with Jimmy, I began to realize there was honor among gamblers, or at least that's how it seemed to me. One day we were walking down the Strip in Las Vegas and a guy who looked like a reprobate came up to Jimmy.

"Jimmy, can you spot me a couple hundred?" the man said.

Jimmy reached into his pocket and gave him the money. I asked why he was doing this and was told to shut up and mind my own business. Jimmy said this was a guy who needed help and was down on his luck and he was going to help him. He also told me not to worry because he knew he would get the money back.

When I pressed him on how he knew it, he told me, "That is for me to know and for you to find out."

After he signed the contract with CBS, we were concerned about the impact of his travel schedule on his health. For that reason, and because Las Vegas is the capital of gambling, we began to talk about moving Jimmy closer to New York. When I asked him where he'd like to live, he said he loved Florida and Connecticut. I knew he loved Florida because of Hialeah Park Racetrack, so that wasn't going to work. He also said he loved Durham, North Carolina, so that's where I started looking for his new home. There were no racetracks, it was a beautiful community, and it was close to New York. Jimmy had been there to take part in a weight-loss program called the Rice Diet at Duke University.

As I was looking at property, Jimmy enrolled in the Rice Diet program for the second or third time.

During that trip, I had the pleasure of meeting Buddy Hackett, who was also at Duke for the diet. He and Jimmy were buddies, and when they were at Duke at the same time, it was pandemonium and absolutely hilarious, with no weight loss going on. In fact, they gained because they'd call out for pizza.

I said, "Guys, it costs 10,000 bucks to bring you in here to go on a goddamn diet and you're cheating?!"

They bribed the orderlies to go out and sneak in forbidden foods, laughing like two little kids. From the couple of times I met Buddy Hackett in person, I can tell you he was the same in person as he was on stage—incredibly funny and a first-class gentleman. And watching Jimmy and Buddy walking together was a classic Mutt and Jeff scene.

We eventually found Jimmy a house in Durham. It belonged to the chairman of the board of the American Tobacco Company who was moving to New York. The house was gorgeous. Roughly 10,000 to 12,000 square feet, it was a tri-level home on two-and-a-half acres, right off the fourteenth hole of the country club golf course. Price tag: $400,000. Being so used to Southern California real estate prices, I asked if something was wrong with the house because the price was so low.

Jimmy bought the house after it passed a thorough inspection, and his wife decorated it beautifully. Joan was a talented and artistic lady who knew how to spend money better than anyone I knew at the time. The two of them collected glass objects by Steuben, and he gave the art pieces as business gifts.

CHAPTER 11

Alpha And Omega Growth Spurt

"The pace of events is moving so fast that unless we can find some way to keep our sights on tomorrow, we cannot expect to be in touch with today."

DEAN RUSK, US SECRETARY OF STATE, 1961-1969

ARLY IN OUR business relationship, I either flew with Jimmy or met him somewhere around the country. This hindered my business development activities in the San Diego market. But as fate would have it, a former coworker at California First Bank, Jim Boyle, called me. He was working at Security Pacific Bank by then and said the bank needed my expertise. When I inquired as to what they were looking for, he said "someone who could provide help to the retirement division of the Trust Department." At the time, Security Pacific was the second-largest bank in the state.

I met with Robert "Bob" H. Smith, executive vice president of the Trust Department, and Richard J. Flamson, chairman of the board of directors. I drove to Los Angeles to meet them, along with several other people associated with the Trust Department. Shortly after I made my presentation, I was retained to do some serious consulting work for them. The project was to help evaluate the existing operations of the pension division, expand their services, and improve their marketing efforts.

The contract I signed was worth close to a quarter of a million dollars. That single introduction financed Alpha & Omega for a number of years and gave us the backing to expand our operation beyond serving only Jimmy. The contract lasted over three years and brought enough income to fund our expansion; it allowed us to start attending some key bank trade shows and expand our marketing efforts within the trust industry. Finally, we were able to get serious with other banks and corporations about consulting.

Despite landing the contract, we were short on cash. The initial $50,000 capital was beginning to look pretty thin, so I went back to the banks for another line of credit. Again, the good Lord guided my path, this time to a marvelous woman named Rita McCoy.

Rita was the first woman to be president of the first women's-chartered bank in San Diego. Shortly after Jimmy Carter was elected president, he reached out to her and made her the number-two person in the Small Business Administration (SBA). When I met Rita, she had left the SBA and come back to San Diego to work for a company called The Money Store. It was there I successfully was able to borrow a quarter of a million dollars.

We now had the cash to finance our activities to handle the work needed for Security Pacific and others. With this money, I was also able to pay off my loan to the Bank of San Diego and hire a dear friend and associate from my days at California First Bank, now Union Bank, Murray Steeg. He was an incredible worker with a strong operations background. Jimmy the Greek and Security Pacific were just the beginning of building Alpha & Omega into a multimillion-dollar business.

By 1980, we had developed a few qualified plan clients. At the same time, I was developing a new concept in the industry, which we marketed as the Ready Retirement System. It was designed to be a full turnkey program for institutions and third-party administrators. The program consisted of various slide show presentations, a prototype plan document, a trust manual, and various plan administration manuals for the plan's sponsor clients of the institution or third-party administrators. We got lucky and started to sell a few copies of this program to several banks at a price of $25,000 a copy and double the price if the client required customization. (Our Ready Retirement System program was instrumental in landing us the consulting contract with Security Pacific.)

We were beginning to develop a good reputation in the trust industry, and by 1982 we landed another contract, this time with a new bank that wanted to establish a Trust Department. The bank was called Bank of San Diego; it was founded by James "Jim" S. Brown, chairman of the board, and Ray Innocenti, chief operations officer, with Lowell Halleck as president. This assignment was far more complex; they wanted us to file an application with state banking authorities to form a Trust Department for the bank, which would fall under the California bank holding company. Such applications are complex and time-consuming. One of the more complex aspects dealt with the preparation of a needs assessment to justify why a Trust Department was appropriate. Along with the needs assessment, we put together an economic analysis demonstrating that such services were in demand in the San Diego market and could be profitable and competitive with the other banks that had Trust Departments.

In those years, there were nine or ten Trust Departments in the city; today there are basically none headquartered in San Diego. In time, the application was submitted, and after about six months the regulators granted the bank a trust charter. Once the charter was granted, we were confronted with developing operational systems and finding the staff to manage the Trust Department. We were glad the Security Pacific contract was coming to an end; that would free our time to work on the San Diego Bank contract, or so we thought.

As the original Security Pacific contract was coming to an end, we were offered another contract, this time to study the possibility of creating a brand-new division under the Trust Department, specializing in plan design, plan administration, and actuarial services.

Murray and I evaluated the potential for Security Pacific to create a different company that would be unique to banking. We analyzed what it would take to find qualified employees to run the company and the requisite background qualifications. We evaluated Security Pacific's ratio of accounts representing business versus individual accounts and the mix of business sizes. Finally, we examined what their banking competitors were doing, if anything, in the area. We discovered the competition was, like Security Pacific, only seeking to manage the assets of pensions and 401(k) plans. Finally, we examined the branch system as a source of lead generation.

Our report concluded, somewhat to our surprise, that the potential revenue from the formation of such a company, if properly organized, could be an extraordinary winner.

Murray and I set our work aside for a few days to let our findings germinate. We also needed to give our minds a rest from the intensity of the effort. After a few days, we picked up our draft and went through it once more with a fine-tooth comb, recognizing that when we delivered our report it was going to be dissected six ways from Sunday.

Once again, we concluded if the company was structured properly, and with the right leadership and systems in place, within three years they would be generating around $30 million a year in gross revenue. The number bothered us; we decided to cut it by 50 percent and sent it to the dynamic duo: Flamson, chairman of the board and Smith, the executive vice president.

When the day came to meet with Smith and Flamson, we took the train to Los Angeles and rehearsed our presentation as we rode. At the meeting, the two men asked several questions about personnel, system needs, and more. The meeting ended with them promising to get back to us.

Almost two months passed before the second meeting. Flamson said according to his internal research team, our gross income projection was very conservative. That made Murray and me very happy. He suggested they were considering next steps, possibly including asking us to prepare a detailed report on staffing needs, operating systems, and characteristics to look for in a leader of this company. (We had built into our original report that if they did not structure the company as we outlined, they would lose up to $10 million.)

Sure enough, they came back asking us to define and prepare job descriptions, including compensation estimates. Our report recommended that the likely candidate should possess fifteen to twenty years of experience in the benefit consulting field, primarily from among the top four firms. To attract a quality candidate to head the company, they would need to offer compensation of $150,000, plus incentives. At that time, banks hesitated to offer big wages, and this number fell in that upper range. What we were proposing touched a sensitive nerve. We also recommended what we felt was the most-user friendly and effective operating system.

We offered to conduct the search process at traditional fees of 30 percent of gross pay. They negotiated us down to 25 percent. I reached out to my close contacts at the major consulting firms in Southern California, describing a company whose sole purpose was to specialize in retirement plan design, consulting, and administration.

After a search, we presented three names. The bank interviewed all three candidates. A long wait ensued. After a couple of months, I couldn't wait any longer, so I called Flamson to ask which candidate they preferred. His response was they were all most impressive, but they had found someone who only required compensation of $75,000—a Mr. Chambers, who also happened to work in their HR Department, in benefits.

I tried to explain that Mr. Chambers was not a salesperson nor was he trained as a benefits consultant, not to mention lacking other critical qualifications. But they went ahead and gave him the position.

It didn't take long to demonstrate that Mr. Chambers was a duck out of water. His first major decision was to buy two competing operating systems that did the same thing. Within two years, the bank came back to us to ask us to help in the search for Mr. Chambers' replacement.

I turned them down because the fledgling company was already developing a negative reputation; none of my contacts would touch it. The bank went out to search on its own. They recruited someone who was head of Kraft Food Benefit Department. He survived long enough to close the doors on the venture.

This experiment ended up costing the bank something like $10 million-plus in losses. Its reputation and prestige as an organization with an understanding of the complexity and significance of pensions was diminished. In fact, to help unwind the company, they retained my good friend, Alex Bruckner, a well-known Los Angeles attorney who specializes in ERISA (Employee Retirement Income Security Act).

Bob Smith, who was then executive vice president of the Trust Department, approached us with the possibility of being bought by them.

By this time, things were picking up with the Bank of San Diego; we were retained to begin locating staffing and systems to operate the Trust Department. Murray and I were experiencing our own operational difficulties; we were falling behind in serving our other clients because the Bank of San Diego was requiring more and more of our time. I recognized if that kept up, we'd be out of business, or the bank would own us by default without having paid us a penny. Murray and I concluded either we break our contract with the bank, they buy us out and we go to work for them, or one of us leaves A & O to work full time with the bank. We chose the last option, and Murray agreed to be the one to go.

My next move was to meet with Lowell Halleck to discuss our dilemma. I laid out the two scenarios that were available to him. He asked me how much I wanted for Alpha & Omega. I said one million dollars and didn't care how they paid me: company stock, cash, or another method. That was not acceptable to him, so I then suggested he hire Murray at a specific salary. That was what he chose. I think Halleck was enough of a businessman to understand we could not sacrifice our other clients at the expense of serving only his needs. Murray went on to become the operations officer of the Trust Department and played a major role in developing it into a thriving operation.

I have to say Murray and I were truly grateful for Security Pacific. They put us on the map and financed our growth and future successes. There are many things I would have done differently, but I am grateful to Jim Boyle, who introduced us and made it possible for us to spend time and effort with the bank.

In the meantime, we were looking for a senior trust officer to head up the bank's Trust Department and recommended another colleague of ours from California First Bank, Don Levi. Don was another incredible individual, a hard worker, very bright with a lot of connections in San Diego. In time, Don and Murray grew the Trust Department with assets equal to one billion dollars under custody. They managed to do that in a matter of a few years, but then the parent company of the Trust Department, the Bank of San Diego, was closed down by the banking regulators. Well, that is another story for another book. Don't worry. Don and Murray went on to form another trust company in partnership with Grossmont Bank. Known as Western Trust, it grew into a multibillion-dollar enterprise before it was closed down by the parent company, Grossmont Bank. The closure was over a lawsuit against the Trust Department brought by various customers who had invested in collateralized trust deeds, where I became its key expert witness. The Trust Department won its case, but the bank was left with such a bad taste it proceeded to close it. The lawsuit cost them millions of dollars. Frankly, it was a sad loss in the city.

CHAPTER 12

The Birth And Growth
Of PenChecks

*"Each morning puts a man on trial and
each evening passes judgement."*

ROY L. SMITH, AMERICAN CLERGYMAN, NEWSPAPER COLUMNIST, AND AUTHOR

A T A 1994 national trade association conference sponsored by the
American Society of Pension Professionals & Actuaries (ASPPA)
held in Washington, DC, several of us were talking, over cocktails
about the new "10,000 pound gorilla" that had entered our space. Historically, our industry had been dominated by TPAs, insurance companies, banks, and actuaries that comfortably coexisted. No one tried
to destroy or take advantage of any of the others; we viewed each other
as equals, all necessary to the business of designing and administering
retirement plans.

The TPAs, sometimes referred to as benefit consultants, worked
with insurance companies and banks. The banks and insurance
companies were all about managing the money that went into these
retirement plans. The third-party administrators and actuaries
designed the plans, did the legal work, and petitioned the IRS to get
approvals to establish a retirement plan for an employer, to make

sure the legal documents met the standards of the Department of Labor and IRS rules and regulations. Each plan needed to be administrated, including preparing the annual tax returns and reporting to the employees what their benefit was worth. This also included calculating retirement benefits; the actuaries did the calculations to ensure the employer contributed the correct amount of money for defined benefit pension and cash balance plans. They also determined whether the retirement plan had sufficient funds in the trust to pay the promised benefits set forth in the plan document approved by the IRS.

In 1978, the world of the retirement industry was about to change forever. Congress passed a law introducing what is today known as the 401(k) plan. It was never intended to replace well-established retirement plans, but merely be a supplement to teach and encourage employees the importance of saving.

Back to the 10,000-pound gorilla, which to that point had virtually no role or impact on the retirement community: the mutual fund industry. They saw this law as having been written specifically for them. Keep in mind that the technology we have today did not exist in 1978. The new law, in creating the 401(k) plan, was structured in such a way as to allow employers to set up plans that let their employees manage their own money. The TPAs and others in the industry yawned, saying, "Who in their right mind would allow their employees to manage their money?"

The mutual fund industry saw it differently; this was a great opportunity. They could provide the participant employees with the opportunity to see how their investments were doing and even change investments by dialing a free, 1-800 number. (Long-distance calls were costly in those days.) The pension industry software suppliers did not jump on the bandwagon initially to write new software to handle these new 401(k) options.

By 1994, the mutual fund industry, with all its money and sales representatives, began pulling in $15 *billion* per *month*. The banks lost their lofty position as the major holders of retirement assets. Today, they control only about 18 percent of all the retirement assets in the country.

The insurance industry quickly reacted to defend their position and continues in a strong second place. They came up with a remarkable strategy of partnering with administrators, actuaries, and registered investment advisors (RIAs). In effect, these entities became the sales force for the insurers. Partners were rewarded for their efforts with fees, vacations, and more.

Whereas the banks and insurance companies played nice and saw third-party administrators and actuaries as allies, the mutual fund industry didn't. They saw them as a necessary evil and if they could go around them, they would, and in many cases they did. Their sole purpose was to grab assets; they didn't even care whether or not the retirement plan was the right plan for the employer. Once they unleashed their marketing and sales team efforts and unlimited marketing budgets, that was the end. By 1986, they had everything in place: marketing materials, trained sales staff, and pre-approved IRS prototype plan documents. They were ready.

Back to my colleagues and me at the conference, bemoaning our plight.

"Why don't a number of us get together and discuss the issues," I suggested. "See if we can come up with some answers on how we might best defend and compete."

Our next step was to identify the parties we wanted at that meeting. We set out to bring together some of the best-operated third-party administration firms in the country. I agreed to host the meeting in Orange County, California over a weekend. We then put together, thanks to the efforts of Jim Christenson, a list of fifty firms and sent out invitations. Jim operated his own TPA firm in Orange City, California.

Of the fifty firms invited, thirty showed up.

At the time, I was a licensed facilitator trained by the Stephen Covey organization. Stephen was the author of a bestselling book, *The Seven Habits of Highly Effective People*. I used those skills to walk everyone through the weekend. We started out by determining we were not competitors, even though we were in the same industry.

Why is that? Because all of us have built our practices, even to this day, via referrals. Once we got past that issue, the floodgates opened, and everyone was willing to share their views.

During that weekend, we talked about what we liked about what we do, and what we disliked about what we do. As was the case in most facilitator experiences conducted at that time, we recorded comments on butcher paper and hung them on the wall.

I asked the group, "Is there anything we dislike and would like to get out of doing?"

On the paper, I listed the things we would like to get out of. I then passed out colored dots: green for first place, red for second, and blue for third. Everyone, without exception, cast the same vote for first place, which was, get out of the distribution business, or the paying of benefits. I had another question.

"Why do you feel that way?"

No one had a real answer. They just instinctively knew it wasn't profitable.

We agreed to put up some money to hire a time-and-motion consultant to visit some of our firms and test what was going on. We chose two large firms, two middle-size firms, and two small firms to be studied. The results were staggering. It took between four to six hours to finally get benefits paid to an individual. When you asked each attendee what they charged, some didn't charge anything, some charged twenty-five dollars, some fifty dollars; only two firms charged one hundred dollars. We suggested they might be breaking even. Today, thanks to technology, this experience has significantly changed.

After all this was discussed and studied, one member named Jim Norman asked the question: "Could you form a company in which their entire focus was on becoming the nation's expert in benefit payment processing, and could it survive?" Well, seventeen firms were willing to put up $10,000 apiece to fund this new entity, called PenChecks, Inc. Jim Norman coined the name of the company.

The original investors were Yvonne Walker, Joyce Annenberg, Robert Carolan, C. James Christenson, Charles E. Johnson, Cheri Kessner, James G. Kreder, James R. Norman Jr., Peter E. Preovolos, Barbara Puccinin, Roger Sherman, James Wagner, Philip H. Weinreich Jr., Peter Zebot, Michael Callahan, Peter Randal Stephen, and James Halinnan.

We prepared projected budgets detailing how long it would take us to break even. Given that no one was doing this yet, we had no point of comparison. We looked at the payroll services industry (firms such as ADP and Paychex) and adopted their model.

The experiment has worked very well. As an example, in 1994 we processed $500,000 in benefits; by 2015 we were processing more than $1.5 billion a year.

PenChecks was not a break-even operation out of the gate. Like most startup ventures, we had to form a corporation. By the second year, we were running short of funds. We lacked a proprietary system, but with some creative thinking, we successfully figured out how to manipulate QuickBooks to suit our needs. (A few years later, some of our full-time employees attended an Intuit training class. As I predicted, the instructor informed them it was not possible to use the system as they described.)

By the end of the second year at PenChecks, we began to assess the original stockholders fifty dollars per month. That lasted about two years. The entire operation was officing in the Alpha & Omega space, and PenChecks was not contributing to the rent or phone services payments.

By our fourth year, a couple of firms pulled out, feeling it was a bad idea and would continue to be a loser. We lost some of the original investors: Carolan, Christenson, Wagner, Weinreich, and Walker. Leaving meant the loss of your seat on the board and forfeiting 400 shares of stock out of the original 500.

In year four, the assessment ended. Our position was that the company had to survive without it. PenChecks was doing four to six trade shows a year by then. In the early days, Jim Norman and I attended the shows. By year seven, Jim Kreder and Joyce Annenberg were joining me in the booths. I'm sorry to say these two fine individuals are both of blessed memory.

Tom Drosky became our first direct sales specialist onsite at the trade shows. He, too, is an incredible person and a tremendous worker whose significant contributions helped put PenChecks on the map.

By April 2015, we had decided to hire a national sales director to develop a sales team. The position went to Scott Okrasinski, a highly qualified professional with an impressive track record. Within two years, the PenChecks sales team grew from what had been only Tom Drosky, Scott, and me to include eight talented people.

Since his arrival, Scott and his team have grown the business by 20 percent per year, including during 2020, the year when the COVID-19 pandemic weakened so many businesses globally. Grounded from calling on existing clients and prospects in person, the team was still able to achieve those results and meet their goals at the end of 2020.

By our fifth year of operation, clients were coming to us for answers to troubling administrative issues. The first one involved locating plan participants who had been terminated from a company but could not be found. We worked with our ERISA counsel, the Los Angeles firm of Farmer & Ridley LLP.

Robert W. "Bob" Ridley, chief counsel for PenChecks, did a great deal of work with the industry in Southern California and at the national level, in particular with the International Foundation of Employee Benefit Plans. An examination of ERISA showed the law did not preclude setting up separate accounts. Since we could find no prohibition against doing that for missing participants, we began working with Ridley to develop an IRA that truly was unique. It contained a provision stating that if there was a beneficiary designation on file, we would attach it to the IRA. If the plan had protected benefits, we would attach that language to the individual's IRA. We restricted the offering to FDIC-insured investments.

As we were developing this program, we asked ourselves how someone would be able to find their money.

The board came up with the idea of forming a public service company called the National Registry of Unclaimed Retirement Benefits (NRURB). If a former plan participant was searching the internet, they would eventually land on the NRURB site. They would be asked to enter their Social Security number, and if there was a match, an information page would come up showing where the money was, who registered them, and how to contact that person. Simultaneously, it sent a notice to the person or organization who registered them, notifying them the participant had been found. Five years later, Congress passed the Default Auto Rollover bill, authorizing employers to move such money into an Auto Rollover Default IRA.

Although we were growing that aspect of the business, some questioned our authority to perform this service. The passage of the new law gave us immediate credibility. However, that part of the law had a sunset provision giving the Department of Labor (DOL) thirty-six months to produce policies and procedures.

About fourteen months after passage of the law, we got a knock on our door. It was a DOL agent who came to audit how we handle this type of business.

At the end of the audit, the agent informed us it didn't appear we cared about finding these missing people to give them their money. I immediately gave him a copy of our brochure on the NRURB, and he walked out.

Shortly after, the DOL published its regulations, which were almost a carbon copy of our policies and procedures.

Within three years, we found ourselves with some formidable competitors who jumped on, offering their own default auto rollover services. The advantage most had over us was a lot of capital, but more importantly they were custodians of retirement plan assets, etc. Their client base gave them a ready market from which to grow that book of business very quickly.

The next significant thing PenChecks introduced was our uncashed check services. If there is a black mark on the industry, it is the tens of billions of dollars sitting in the banks, insurance, and brokerage firms of uncashed retirement payments. Very few people in the industry had any real experience in this space. Perhaps I was fortunate to have been exposed to this problem back in the 1960s when I was a trust officer at Wells Fargo working in the Pension Department.

Bear in mind this was pre-ERISA, a federal law signed by President Gerald Ford in 1974. ERISA sets minimum standards for most voluntarily established retirement and health plans in private industry to provide protection for individuals in these plans.

At the time, I was the senior trust officer administering the corporate accounts for clients such as Bechtel Corporation, MJB Coffee, and Levi Strauss. Every year, their outside professionals would perform an audit of their plans and review all transactions within thirty days following completion of the audit. They would then send a letter to me identifying any issues they uncovered; in most cases, the biggest one was uncashed checks. The letter listed all the uncashed checks in date order, dollar amount, and the computed interest Wells Fargo had to pay to each participant for sitting on their money. Wells paid each participant the interest calculated by the auditors.

The auditors' instructions were that once you credited each person their interest, the funds should be returned to the plan. Wells never objected; they understood their fiduciary obligation. I don't want to paint them lily white. Unless it was called to their attention, they did not search their records looking for such cases and uncashed checks.

I spoke to the DOL about this problem over the years. After a decade of discussion, they began adding this question to their audit examination proceedings checklist. The one thing they haven't done, and it is certainly within their power, is to force the institution to pay interest to the participant as Wells Fargo did.

We were retained to pay benefits from a very large terminated 401(k) plan valued at $60 million. The assets were custodied by one of the top five mutual fund companies. After we finished making all the payments, the attorneys of the terminated plan completed their filing with the IRS.

This was done to obtain approval to terminate. The mutual fund company writes to the plan sponsor to ask what they want to do with some two hundred uncashed checks. The plan sponsor suggested they contact us, which they did, but they never retained us to help them. To this date, I have no idea what they did.

Today, PenChecks processes tens of millions of dollars of uncashed checks for the industry.

One of the unique features for those who process benefit payments through PenChecks is a guarantee that every uncashed check will be addressed and resolved. The recipient is thus protected from losing income.

Since we started offering this uncashed check service to institutions that are custodians of retirement plans, we have processed close to $200 million in uncashed checks. Many of the checks we have received were written twenty to thirty years ago.

One of the challenges occurs when institutions merge, as uncashed checks tend to get lost in the merger process. Clearly, there is a need for better tracking systems to catch a check that has gone uncashed. The amount of money these institutions collectively hold in uncashed checks is in the hundreds of millions, if not billions.

At PenChecks, we have been able to locate about 20 percent of those participants whose funds are older than three to four years. For those whose checks have been uncashed for less than three years, our "find ratio" is closer to 50 percent. Obviously, the possibility of funds being reunited with the rightful owners diminishes over time, which creates a critical need for a system to monitor these transactions.

As I look back over the twenty-six years I was at the helm of PenChecks, my single disappointment was the industry's hesitation to use NRURB—a no-fee public service company. Plan administrators have a fiduciary responsibility to identify missing or non-responsive participants; this has been clearly spelled out by the DOL.

In my opinion, the regulations do not go far enough. Following the regulations and adopting a policy to register all missing, non-responsive participants in the database of NRURB would close the loop in attempting to locate those individuals and satisfy the fiduciary work standard.

Senator Elizabeth Warren talked about a National Registry. I wrote her to explain her idea was good, but such a registry exists. I offered to transfer the ownership rights and software to the federal government to own it and operate if she was totally committed to her idea. I heard nothing back from her except a letter saying we appreciate your support.

I was cheered to see Senator Warren (D-MA) and Steve Daines (R-MT) introduce the bipartisan Retirement Savings Lost and Found Act in 2018, reintroduce it in 2020, and again in 2021.

Finally, regarding this subject, there are many things the industry could do to virtually eliminate this problem. I have lectured about solutions before various groups. The key solution, in my opinion, is for the TPA community to realize they are the gatekeepers, and they have the most up-to-date information on each distribution. For instance, when a distribution is to be processed, the TPA prepares all the paperwork and release forms for plan participants to begin the process of paying out.

I have suggested that once a quarter they communicate with the custodian(s) of each of their clients' plans to provide a list of all payments requested that have not been cashed. This would show which checks have not cleared, enabling the plan sponsor to attempt to locate the person in question right away.

Some institutions have made major strides in developing systems to monitor uncashed checks and send a list of them to the plan sponsor quarterly. For example, John Hancock has such a program. If all institutions would do this, it would have a significant impact on reducing the uncashed check problem.

I've been asked many times what I believe was the single contributing factor to PenChecks' success. My answer is three specific things, starting with PenChecks' employees, who are committed to offering a great service to the industry.

Second, without a doubt, is the magnificent founding board of directors. Every one of the board members owned their own TPA firms, with the exception of Mark Simmons, a former bank president. These individuals weren't out to satisfy their egos, but to form a company to create a series of solutions to issues that would enable us to be more efficient and profitable. When discussing issues at a board level, you had people who understood the problems, what it meant to be a fiduciary, and what it takes to be the caretaker of other people's money. What was perhaps more amazing was that each member held a particular specialty in the pension field. Each brought a depth of understanding of the administrative experience and the issues confronting those in the field.

The original PenChecks board of directors fully appreciated the unique nature of the industry we work in, the pitfalls, and the need to maintain the highest fiduciary standards at all times. They collectively had approximately 400 years of experience in the field, and our management team benefited from their strong support.

The current PenChecks board of directors includes highly professional individuals whose industry backgrounds may be more limited than those of the original board, but their business skills and insight have helped the company grow in size, profitability, and value. The original board was the right board at the right time. The current board members are well positioned to direct the business of the company.

The third major contributor to the continued success of PenChecks is communication. When people or groups in the same industry are willing to let their hair down and openly discuss problems, it is amazing what can come out of it. I believe PenChecks is an example of that theory in action.

CHAPTER 13

Changing The World, One Child At A Time

"The dance, of all the arts, is the one that most influences the soul. Dancing is divine in its nature and is the gift of the gods."
PLATO

IN SEPTEMBER 1823, an article appeared in the British journal, *The Adventurer of the Nineteenth Century.* Titled "The Greek Dance," the author penned: "I was riveted to the ground this evening and positively unable to move so long as the exhibition lasted...I was actually enchanted at the elegance which displayed itself in every movement and which is assuredly not surpassed by anything I have ever witnessed on the Parisian and German stages."

The awe that Greek dancing inspired wasn't simply a phenomenon experienced by the nineteenth century tourist. The dance, as an integral part of Greek culture, dates back to antiquity. Dance was part of an education that included music and writing. Socrates, the great philosopher, believed every man should know how to dance to keep his body strong and flexible—ready for trials on the field of battle.

In ancient times, dancing was done to ensure fertility, cure illness, express joy, and celebrate religious festivals, or in preparation to go into battle. Today, villages throughout the far-flung Greek isles and mainland continue the traditions of old. Every dance has a story to tell and Greek dancing keeps those stories alive, whether the dancer acts out the wild battlefield movements from Crete and Pontos or the slow, heavy rhythms of Epirus.

But how did the dances that were so much a part of early Greece become my story? That's a story in itself.

THE FOLK DANCE FESTIVAL (FDF) IS BORN

In the early 1970s, the local San Diego Greek community at St. Spyridon Greek Orthodox Church on Park Boulevard started hosting an annual food festival. As part of the entertainment, a group of dancers would come from Los Angeles or Oakland to entertain during the festival.

In 1975, I became the youth director at St. Spyridon, supervising the Junior Parish Council (JPC). This was a youth group made up of teenagers and young adults in the parish who were being trained in church duties and parish council administration.

The young people of our parish and the JPC members in particular, had also begun to take a serious interest in Greek dance. In fact, as far back as 1959, the youth of St. Spyridon were learning and performing traditional dances of Greece.

Beginning in the 1970s, many of them were inspired by the weekly folk dance classes held in the parish hall, which were open to anyone in the San Diego community. In 1972, a couple named Don and Ellie Hiatt had taken over the classes from Betty and Jerry Garies, who had volunteered to teach the Zorba Dancers from St. Spyridon.

Don and Ellie were responsible for teaching the classes at the time, and recruited other accomplished teachers, including Greek dance experts. Through these classes, and their own Greek family backgrounds, several young adults who were on the Junior Parish Council had become enthusiastic Greek dance learners.

One day some of the dancers asked about performing at the church festival. They had been performing locally at shopping malls, retirement homes, and other venues. There wasn't a good reason why they couldn't do this, except some adults in the church weren't sure their skills were on a festival-performance level.

I gathered the teens and young adults of the JPC to discuss their request to dance at the annual food festival. We also talked about dancing as a way of meeting other young Greek men and women. Don and Ellie supported the idea of performing at the food festival, as well as using dance as a way to bring kids together. In my role as treasurer of the St. Spyridon Parish Council at the time, I promised to use whatever influence I had to advocate for their goal.

The food festival and the dance competition idea seemed to have some synergy. The members of the JPC formed a group called the Aegean Dancers. They were the first to look beyond the classic or traditional dances of Greece, pursuing some of the more difficult dances from various regions and developing regional costumes.

From 1974 to 1980, the members of the Aegean Dancers were Nicky Adams, Connie Angeles-Thomas, Nick Athan, John Basdakis, Zino Basdakis, Earl Cantos, Roxanne Cantos, Athene Deneris, George Fahouris, Diane Gallanis, Patricia Gallanis, Themis Gallanis, Christine Gotses, Marilyn Kromydas, Garland Merfield, Ann Pitzer, Madelynn Rigolopoulos, George Scarvelis, Jeanne Scarvelis, Tina Stassis, Barbara Stephanos, Christine Trompas, and Dave Weil. These dedicated dancers practiced hard and performed at the food festival. Tony Demopoulos and Trish Musgraoz joined soon after. Those two eventually married.

We talked about how my suggestion of putting together a competitive folk-dance festival, which came to be called FDF, coincided with the Aegean Dancers' passion for performing. From those discussions, FDF was born.

The fire of the Greek Orthodox Folk Dance Festival (FDF) had been lit. The flame was sparked in those Friday night dance classes, at the church festivals, and in my desire for our kids to meet kids from other Greek communities in the western US.

Here is an excerpt from a 2015 interview with George Scarvelis, one of the original members of the Aegean Dancers.

"The Aegean Dancers invited the Festival Dancers from Oakland's Ascension Cathedral to perform at the Greek Bazaar in 1976. The Festival was a very talented group of dancers, part of a larger ensemble that included singers and musicians under the direction of Perry Phillips. The Aegeans and the Festival performers had so much chemistry that the idea was born. 'How do we get this to happen on a bigger scale, with more groups, and specifically for Greek dance?'

That initial spark grew into a flame that's never been quenched. Most of us that were involved at that time were second-generation Greek-Americans. The power of that idea was a desire to connect, then to show off, to impress, but really to share a common pride and love of our shared heritage."

Nothing Happens By Accident

The seeds of FDF were planted a few years before we arrived in San Diego. My wife and I attended an event at the Rose Bowl sponsored by the Mormon Church (The Church of Jesus Christ of Latter-day Saints). The event featured close to 5,000 teenagers in the stadium, all square dancing.

I turned to my wife and said, "Can you imagine 5,000 Greek kids in Greek costumes performing Greek dances?"

At that time, I couldn't imagine moving to San Diego, let alone becoming the youth director for St. Spyridon.

As a note of congratulations, George's daughter, Stamatia Scarvelis, competed in the Women's Hammer Throw in the Tokyo 2020 Olympics, held in 2021 due to the pandemic. Born and raised in the US, Stamatia represented Greece, thanks to dual cititzenship through her grandparents. Amazing young woman.

Although some counties have more than one Greek community, at the time St. Spyridon was the only one in San Diego. The next closest community was St. John's Greek Orthodox Church in Anaheim, and there was virtually no interaction between the two communities.

Los Angeles had a number of Greek Orthodox churches that formed basketball and volleyball leagues where kids from different Orthodox churches could come, meet one another, and compete. Our kids at St. Spyridon felt isolated from their fellow Greek

Orthodox young people and were too far away to effectively be part of the sports activities.

There was much debate over the competition; some of the young adults who loved Greek dancing felt it would be irreverent or even blasphemous to put Greek dancing into a competitive arena. Other options seemed less interesting or likely to provide a reason to come to San Diego.

In fact, competition caused a great deal of pushback. But without the competitive element, FDF would not have grown from its original thirty-nine dancers and five teams to 2,000 kids and 110 teams at its most popular. Competition was the stimulus that got people excited about FDF. Kids and their parents learned that Greek dancing wasn't just those dances we all grew up learning: Hasapiko, Sirtos, Tsamikos, and Kalamatiano.

As the concept of FDF unfolded, I also began to see the power of using it as a teaching tool, not just to develop and perfect dancing skills and teach the history of dance. Dance was a way to introduce best business practices, organizational skills, budgeting, and negotiation. What an opportunity for our young people!

Orthodox Form of Junior Achievement

If you don't believe God works in mysterious ways, you should reconsider, for in my opinion nothing happens by accident. The seeds were planted and would one day germinate at the right time and place.

Also, while working in San Francisco for Wells Fargo Bank, I was assigned by Wells to be an advisor to one of the Junior Achievement groups. It was an amazing experience. In a way, FDF became the Greek Junior Achievment.

THE MISSION OF FDF

The mission of FDF was two-pronged.

Greek folk dancing is primarily done in a circle, moving counter-clockwise while holding the hands of the person on either side of you. That team aspect also translated to the other prong, which was the sense of community—bringing people together. It may be the greatest support program on Earth.

Teaching the importance of teamwork, for me, meant showing our kids that if you want a business to succeed, you must be willing to learn the ropes and do your part—best business practices, the ethics and challenges of doing business, proper planning, budgeting, and so forth.

Our kids needed to be as committed to the business side as they were to the dance side. In fact, dance is a great example of teamwork, perhaps more subtle than business, but nevertheless it requires teamwork to perform the dance in all of its glory of movement and expression.

In this case, the actual tool for gathering the young adults and teens was learning to do Greek dances as a competitive team.

FDF'S TEACHERS

Although I had the initial idea for FDF, it couldn't have survived even the first year without the help of many people, especially not without the enthusiastic embrace of the young people. We realized early on that to run a successful program, we needed to find people who were connected with the international folk dance community not just Greek folk dancers.

My goal was to identify people who had dedicated their lives to the profession of teaching folk dancing; of course, Greek dancing had to be a part of their repertoire. The first two people who became involved with the program were Don and Ellie, neither of whom was Greek, but in their hearts, they were fellow Hellenes. You couldn't have known two more loving, generous, and giving human beings. They ultimately became FDF's greatest champions and my lifesavers, and part of the heart and soul of FDF.

Both Don and Ellie were great fans of international folk dancing as well as Greek dance. They traveled all over the world to places like Bulgaria, Romania, Greece, Turkey, and Serbia, learning the regional dances. What was wonderful about them is that they could go into a village for any kind of gathering and join the circle of dancers. This opened all kinds of doors for them. They didn't even have to speak the language, but because they could dance, they were embraced as members of the community.

Don and Ellie weren't just instrumental in helping us learn the dances; they also introduced me to people who could be called on to be judges and help us formulate the program. Soon, others in their group who were passionate about folk dancing began to teach our kids. Don and Ellie's connections brought people from LA, as well as the western and eastern parts of the US, who were experts in the various forms of Greek dancing.

THE LEADERSHIP PROGRAM

Business and community are the elements associated with dance and the creation of FDF. The dance brought people together, emphasizing teamwork, discipline, and trying to reach a level of perfection.

In the Orthodox Church, we talk about *theosis*, meaning "Godlike, but not God." The goal is to try to emulate, to achieve a level of *theosis* or perfection. Therefore, the standard has been set by the church in anything we undertake: to seek perfection, to do the best you can in whatever you undertake. The concept is ingrained in us culturally and religiously. So, excelling is in our DNA; we have never been afraid to compete or afraid to step out and try something new.

An integral part of FDF was the leadership program, referred to as GOLD, for Greek Orthodox Leadership Development. I felt it was critical for the young people to learn how to run a business. I wanted them to learn about budgets, how to deal with vendors, and how to go about selecting venues, in addition to dancing. For FDF, that meant putting together a management team of about twenty young people from the ages of fourteen to twenty-one. Every year we'd select from the management team a group who would be held over and go into what we called the Senior Management Team (SMT). These young people truly were the best of the best. To be selected meant you had demonstrated leadership and intellectual skills.

It wasn't always easy to make those choices. Every young person I dealt with was an outstanding individual who you couldn't help but love and respect. We wanted everyone to work hard in anticipation of being selected to serve on the SMT.

The SMT gave the program continuity from year to year and was our way of keeping the knowledge base intact and transferable. In essence, it was the mechanism of passing it forward. Its foundation has allowed it to continue to exist.

The SMT program:

- Operated strictly like a business
- Assigned each person on the team a specific role to perform
- Gave members responsibility for an activity's budget
- Measured results using the PERT (Program Evaluation Review Technique)

Each of the team members had a PERT chart, which identifies the tasks needed to reach an end goal. The team members gathered and each one gave a status report, with progress tracked on a master PERT chart. The chart measured time and tasks, letting team members see the progress of the task and the date required for completion. This approach enabled the team to stay on track and meet goals and objectives to deliver a high-quality program.

This also kept everyone accountable. If anyone fell behind, it was reported to the team. This wasn't about finger-pointing, but about helping the team members help one another. The PERT system was invaluable in identifying where the weakness might be in our process, as well as in building teamwork.

We also sent one of the senior advisors to the Stephen Covey organization to learn leadership skills and share their training with us. The FDF community was blessed to have Geraldine "Gerrie" Magers, chief deputy director of the Health and Welfare Data Center for the state of California from 1987–1999, volunteer to help us in the development of the GOLD program.

I made a point of learning what I could about the people in the senior leadership positions, and often wrote letters to their employers or teachers. These letters explained what their student or employee was doing relative to FDF. I wanted everyone to understand the important role these young people were filling.

Along with the letter, I sent a copy of the budget and a breakdown of the entire operation, describing the complexity and seriousness of the program. I also extended an invitation for them to attend the annual event as our guests.

In 1989, a twenty-four-year-old young lady named Amy Kotsiomitis, from the Oakland community, was our executive director. An incredible young woman and extremely talented, Amy had started dancing at FDF in 1979, the first year the Ascension Cathedral in Oakland sent a team.

> *In those days, we had the FDF in different locations and the home parishes of that location were very involved. Basically, it was my job to join the FDF governing board with my home parish and put together a team to run the event. We were coming out of a year that didn't do so well financially. The 1988 FDF had some issues. There was a lot of focus on budget, being responsible as far as where we were spending our money, setting a package price that was going to ensure that we were going to at least break even, maybe make a little money. I pulled in a lot of people who had experience in budgeting and running a business.*
>
> AMY KOTSIOMITIS STAMISON

Amy had started working for Dreyer's Ice Cream when she was twenty years old. At the time, I'm not sure Dreyer's saw her as being executive material.

I wrote to Amy's boss, as well as to the president of the company, explaining Amy's duties as executive director. Both the president of the company and her boss accepted our invitation to attend FDF that year. Afterward, they told me they had no idea Amy was such a talented young lady.

"I thought it was just going to be a part-time job to get me through college and then I would do something else," Amy recalled. "They offered me a full-time job after I graduated, and I stayed on. Then I started getting involved in the management of FDF. They were all very aware of what I was doing. Because of my success there, I was offered a position in finance."

Today, Amy is a financial analyst at Dreyer's Grand Ice Cream in Oakland, California and a proud parent of FDF dancers.

Amy is one of many examples of young people who achieved success, thanks to their experience in the program. FDF inspired young people and gave them the confidence to go out and create a business of their own or have a high level of confidence in working for a company. Our purpose was to give each member of the team the skills to be possibility thinkers, to understand they could achieve anything if they put their mind to it.

Another wonderful early participant was Loula Moschonas, the daughter of a Greek Orthodox priest from Tucson, Arizona. Loula was involved with FDF early on, both as a dancer, then a teacher, and later as a member of the leadership team. She is still active in FDF to this day.

> I was a teenager when I started, well into my twenties when I took over the finances. It was a learning experience. Peter was always the guiding hand. Litsa, and Don and Ellie: Great mentors, and everything was done as an organization, as a group. Lots of good communication. I think the focus was on kids and building them up so that they could take on leadership positions in the future. That's an excellent concept. That was Peter's concept. At the time, the Metropolitan loved it. Metropolitan Anthony couldn't get enough of it. He was all about the kids, the youth of the diocese. Fulfilling orthodoxy, promoting it so you have the next generation of Greek Orthodox so they wouldn't leave the church. He did that with the carrot of folk dancing and culture.
>
> LOULA MOSCHONAS

Loula is an engineer by profession. She eventually became part of the FDF Advisory Board—our version of a board of trustees. Her contributions in terms of outreach and being an ambassador of the program were invaluable.

"I'm an aerospace consultant now," she said. "I started out as an electrical engineer and I made it all the way to the vice president of space programs operations in one company, to have a twenty-year career there. It was by learning from the mentors I had at FDF."

Unfortunately, under today's leadership, only young adults ages twenty and above are allowed to be part of the team. The adults have done what adults tend to do when they get involved with youth activities, which is to take over. There's a fear the children might make a mistake or fail at their assignment.

One of my few rules during my thirty-five years at FDF was that it was okay to make a mistake, as long as it wasn't repeated. I remember one fourteen-year-old asking me why I would keep someone on the team after they made a mistake. My response was that if a person learned from a mistake, they became even more valuable to the entire program. Embracing the person not as a failure but as one who has learned a great lesson, they became even stronger and more successful.

LEADERSHIP STRUGGLES

In all my years at FDF, I had to remove only one person from the team for not following the rules. It was a difficult decision. The young man was bright and capable, but his arrogance got in the way. We became concerned when several of his friends wanted to quit because he was dismissed. We sat everyone down and tried to teach another lesson: Don't make someone else's problem yours by joining his cause or falling on his sword. We knew those who followed him would learn from the experience, as would those who chose to stay.

A couple of the young man's friends did resign, but years later they realized their resignation had served no purpose other than to cheat themselves of the experience of being on the team and completing the project.

Our son, Spiro G. Preovolos, described FDF like this in an interview. "Dad's original ideal and dream for FDF was that it would be a leadership training program, as well as a type of cultural preservation and religious and spiritual indoctrination program."

Some parents questioned the decision to allow young people to manage a project with a $750,000 annual budget. I believe that kind of doubt says you have trouble trusting your children. They're going to make mistakes and they may not make the same decisions you might make, but how else are they going to learn? The amazing thing is, financially, we succeeded every year, and only twice did we experience close calls.

Of course, we had built-in, fail-safe provisions and practices the team had to follow, especially when it came to certain contract and budgeting issues. In those instances, any changes to those provisions had to come before the advisory board that oversaw the program. We weren't going to let the kids, or the church get into any trouble.

We never had a serious financial problem where the young people were involved. The local communities knew they were to stay out of the decision-making process, since it was in the hands of the kids. The only major loss occurred the last year we allowed local communities to play a significant role in running the program. That experience convinced us to sponsor the annual event independently of the communities. The loss was the result of the community convincing us they had a better budget plan. It ended up costing them $35,000.

Another leadership controversy took place one year when FDF was held in the Northwest. I was there, attending one of the many pre-meetings, asking the bright young girl who served as executive director questions about the process and the progress. She was hesitant in answering, constantly looking at her father.

Turning to her father, I said, "Who's running the show, are you, or is she?"

Then I asked her, "Can you make a decision about anything without consulting your father?"

"No," she said, and hung her head.

I'm sorry to say I lost it. I ripped her father down one side and up the other.

"How despicable that you don't trust your twenty-one-year-old daughter and give her the freedom to succeed or fail at anything. You've taken that opportunity away from her."

It was disappointing and sad to see that a parent would cheat their own child of the experience and opportunity. How shortsighted and selfish of him, afraid that if she failed, he would be embarrassed. In the end, she proved to be a champion who demonstrated leadership and the ability to make decisions. She and her team put on a quality event.

You can tell I feel strongly about this. I want parents to wake up and let their children demonstrate that they have the capacity to succeed. Tell your kids you have faith in them, point them in the right direction, and then let them go. I've never been disappointed by any kid or young adult I've worked with, except one. The only reason I was disappointed in him was he let his ego get in the way. We need a measured amount of ego to get through the minutiae of everyday life. It's like spice on food—don't let it be the dominant factor in your life.

THE COMPETITION

The FDF competition had three parts: the qualifying round, the semifinal round, and the final round.

The qualifying round consisted of demonstrating that you had the ability to dance the three basic Greek dances: the Sirto, Tsamiko, and Kalamatiano. The judges also assigned dancers to an appropriate category. Greek costumes were not worn in this round.

After three or four years, it became apparent the dancers knew how to perform basic and traditional dances. We restructured the competition, creating new classifications, four in each of the two divisions.

The upper classifications in Division I consisted of Intermediate, Advanced Intermediate, Senior, and Advanced Senior. In Division

II, the lower classifications were called Primary, Advanced Primary, Junior, and Advanced Junior.

Groups in each classification had to perform a semifinal round and a final round over two-and-a-half days of competition. Traditionally, in the semifinal round a team performed a series of dances they had performed as their final set the previous year. Their new set of dances would be performed in the current year's final round.

In the early years of FDF it was expected that the final round represented serious research on new dances from regions that hadn't been explored; this gave teams the opportunity to bring these dances back to share with the other competitors. This was one of the major contributors in building the repertoire of well over five hundred different dances performed over the years at FDF.

Naturally, I took great pride in watching our groups at St. Spyridon practice. I was always pushing for excellence, but even more for our kids to learn new dances and the history behind them.

In 1981, our Advanced Senior group, the Aegeans, said they weren't going to let me observe their rehearsals because they wanted their dance to be a complete surprise. I thought that was great but was I curious; my anticipation was huge.

FDF took place in San Jose that year. St. Spyridon's Aegean Dancers performed in the Advanced Senior category and came onto the floor wearing a costume I'd never seen. I'm willing to bet that 90 percent of the audience hadn't seen it either.

The costume was from an area called Pontos. Historically, the Pontians come from Asia Minor, the northern reaches of Greece. The male costume was royal blue with gold piping and the head covering was made of the same material, with gold braids hanging from the crown and sides. Without a doubt, the effect was as if you were watching warriors from a bygone era before going into battle.

The Pontics were known for their warlike determination and commitment to Greek independence. They had a reputation for being fearless. In a Pontic dance, there's so much emotional power. It gives a sense of someone getting ready for battle, which is exactly what is portrayed.

Our team came out and performed their dance. Bishop Anthony and I were sitting in the bleachers, watching in amazement. The bishop knew the dance and the region it was from immediately.

Suddenly, to my right an elderly man started to cry. I immediately

The Kotsari is a popular Pontic Greek dance from the Kars region. Sometimes called a "war dance," Kotsari was originally danced by males, but later, women joined in dance.
PHOTO CREDIT: The Folkway Project by Propantos, Thessaloniki, Greece

went over to him, thinking he might be ill or there was something seriously wrong.

I asked him in Greek, "What's the matter? Are you okay?"

"I now can die," he said, "because I know the spirit of my people lives on."

He was a Pontic and hadn't seen a Pontic dance for decades. At the time he was in his late eighties.

When the kids finished their performance, the audience was silent; the kids didn't even get much open applause. Why?

Some people in the audience came up to the bishop and said, "How dare you allow Turkish dancing here!"

The bishop said, "It shows you how little you know about your own history. This is Greek dancing. Probably some of the most powerful in all of Greece."

The kids got off the stage, barely able to take in the reaction of the audience. I ran down to the dancers and embraced them.

"I thought this was a magnificent and inspiring performance and how very proud I am of you," I said.

The crowd's reaction led to a serious discussion among the team members. I asked them if they had come here to win a medal or to showcase something new. I suggested they might consider forgoing the rules of the competition and returning to the stage for their final round in the same costumes and again perform their preliminary round. I left the group, saying I would learn of their decision tomorrow, at the same time as everyone else, when they stepped onto the dance floor.

The next day when the final competition started, when it was time for the Aegean team to perform, they all came out in the same costumes and repeated the dance.

An amazing thing happened—the audience went crazy with a standing ovation; many attendees had tears in the eyes. Bishop Anthony got up and ran to the microphone. He told the audience the history of the Pontic people and their sacrifices to gain independence from the Ottoman Turks. His commentary made the entire experience even more poignant and inspiring.

That was the beginning of seeing many groups year after year learning and performing Pontic dances. There is a routine in one of the Pontic dances where the men raise their hands with clenched fists and march off. For years, every time other dancers saw our Aegean team, they honored them by raising their hands in the same way.

Much of the credit for the FDF dancers' passion and facility for Pontic dance goes to Nikos Savvidis, who conducted dance workshops, directed performing groups, and became a judge at FDF in 1985. Born in Chrysoupolis, near Kavala, Greece, Nikos' roots are in Pontian culture, dance, and folklore. As a young teenager, he lived in Athens, where he learned to dance in the tavernas. He was a member of the acclaimed Dora Stratou Dance Theatre in Athens and toured Greece, Europe, and Asia.

Today, FDF probably has the largest collection of Greek dances performed anywhere—well over 500 different dances have been performed. These kids have not only embraced them but researched their appropriate costumes as well. In essence, the kids brought the dances back to life.

Without the stimulus of competition, would the level and quality of dance have reached the level of sophistication it has? The pursuit of excellence is a powerful and dynamic force, and it should be encouraged at all times in everything we attempt to do.

What these dancers did—in fact, what all the FDF dancers did—was to preserve the dances from all over Greece, and thus preserve a part of Greek history and culture. If you travel to Greece today, you will witness the locals dancing dances specific to their village. That's part of what makes Greece such a beautiful experience and unique in the world of folk dancing. A village's identity is expressed in dance and music and often has its own story to tell.

Why Competition Works

Another argument in favor of competition: The national church sponsors an oratorical competition in all the metropolises, and the winner of each age group goes to the national competition. They are able to choose from a series of religious topics to develop their presentation. Various parishes embrace this form of competition.

There's a terrific emotional feeling when performing both in a village setting and on a stage in front of an audience. Putting on a regional costume, practicing dance, and then immersing yourself in the experience awakens the spirit of your ancestors and ensures their memory will not be forgotten.

JUDGING THE COMPETITION

Judging any type of dance is a subjective process. There is no final standard saying the way a step is performed is the best and most accurate.

- It is what the judges see with their eyes at that moment.

- It's what they are feeling about how the dance is being performed relative to how it is performed in the village of origin.

- Judges are affected by the costume and how the costume flows as a body moves in rhythm with the music.

- They are influenced by the leader and the dancer at the end.

- The judges want to see the dance team wearing the appropriate costume for that dance.

- Is the line of dancers balanced?

- As the judging criteria evolves, it still involves style, *kefi* (joy, spirit), and presentation.

All these components are going to affect the judging. Add to that the judges' own biases. If they're familiar with that dance and they perceive the dance wasn't danced the way *they* danced it, that's a negative.

Judges were allowed to instruct teams before the competition began if a team invited them to help, a practice that continues today. In the past, judges were required to step away from teaching during the two months prior to FDF; that may not be the case today.

THE CHURCH AND FDF

One year I was in Seattle to promote FDF at St. Demetrios Greek Orthodox Church, in the hope that the parish would become involved. Rev. Homer Demopulos, of blessed memory, was the *proistamenos* (senior parish priest) or pastor of St. Demetrios. He was one of the best-known and highly respected priests in Seattle, and beloved by his parishioners. I gave my presentation to Father Homer and a group of adults who were interested in folk dancing.

Father Homer asked, "What does dance have to do with the Greek Orthodox Church?"

I thought about it for a moment, and responded, "Nothing and yet everything."

St. Demetrios parish joined FDF and to this day, participates avidly. Father Homer was one of its great supporters.

To better explain where Father Homer was coming from when he questioned the role of Greek dance in Greek Orthodoxy, here is an excerpt from his 1993 *Seattle Times* obituary:

> *A few years ago, he [Father Homer] said that, while young people may be seeking change and innovation, "I feel we should come to understand the meaning of tradition, the ongoing life of the Holy Spirit within the church. There is nothing wrong with seeking change, but from what to what?*[1]

The FDF program gathers people closer to the church and the community. What better way to allow a parish priest to impart Christian principles and the faith, and to allow our children and young adults to gather in a wholesome environment?

BEYOND DANCE: FELLOWSHIP AND LEARNING

Another year when we were to host FDF in San Diego, the team member in charge of recruiting an inspirational speaker wrote to the Reverend Billy Graham. Rev. Graham wrote back, thanking him for the opportunity and expressing that our program sounded exciting and inspiring. Rev. Graham could not attend, but recommended we invite the head of the Campus Crusade for Christ, now an international organization known as "Cru" in the US.

The representative came to FDF, where he proved to be quite an inspirational speaker; the kids loved what he had to say. After the presentation, our guest speaker approached Metropolitan Anthony and said, "Your Eminence, I hope you and the Orthodox Church appreciate and understand the power of this mousetrap that you have. I'd give my right arm for something like this."

That was the turning point in Metropolitan Anthony's attitude toward the FDF program. Up until then, he'd been on the fence. Part of his hesitation was that a number of priests were giving him negative feedback: the program was too big, gave the wrong message, and took away from other church activities. But from that moment on, nothing anybody could say or do would change his mind or his attitude or discourage him about the value of FDF. Metropolitan Anthony became the Saint Paul of FDF. No matter where he went in the world, he talked about FDF and its merits. For me, he became the greatest partner I could have ever wished for.

Metropolitan Anthony Gergiannakis died at the age of 69 on December 25, 2004, after a brief illness. May his memory be eternal.

THAT'S ENTERTAINMENT

Anyone working around young people knows they have more energy than any ten adults put together. So, we started having after-competition dances, bands, presentations, and games within a carnival environment, all for the sole purpose of occupying these young people.

Naturally, the kids were in charge of booking and organizing the "acts" that were to entertain at FDF. Our oldest son, Thanasi, was selected to be the executive director of the management team in 1991.

"I've got to tell you my dad was either brilliant or reckless or both, I'm not sure which one it was," Thanasi said. "Because you put a nineteen-year-old in charge of a $400,000 budget, and honestly he did not get in the way of that. It was, this is your job and you need to take care of that and that was the way it worked. We then dispersed that out to the people who were there."

In 1989, Louis Kades from the Cathedral of St. Sophia parish in Los Angeles danced at FDF for the first time. Two years later, Louis headed the FDF management team's entertainment committee for FDF. He was all of thirteen or fourteen years old.

Louis's goal was to turn the Grand Ballroom at the Westin Bonaventure Hotel, where FDF would be held, into a beach party with real sand, palm trees, and beach chairs. Thanasi thought the idea was spectacular, as did the rest of his team.

I said, "Oh, go for it. See if you can do it." All the while I was certain the hotel would nix the idea.

The hotel brought in engineers to see if the floor could handle the weight of the sand. After analyzing the ballroom, the engineers gave the go-ahead.

"We basically got the Beach Boys to agree to do a concert for us, no charge," Louis said. "The only thing was that the expense of putting on the concert was something like $30,000. It was just completely out of our budget, so the moral of the story is we got the Beach Boys, we could have booked them, but we didn't have the budget at that time to do it."

We had sand and palm trees delivered, and while it wasn't the actual Beach Boys, a Southern California band came and performed. The kids were wild with excitement.

That was probably the epitome of bringing together all kinds of outside activities to entertain the attendees. By the way, they got the *Comedy Store* to come and perform each night as well, for the adult attendees.

EXORCISM? YES, EXORCISM

I believe it was that same year when Thanasi and Louis wanted to bring a magic show to perform at FDF, specifically, the acclaimed magician David Copperfield.

Louis wrote to Copperfield's agent, who wrote back to say if the dates of a New York engagement didn't conflict with FDF, David would be honored to accept the invitation.

It turned out Copperfield was unable to make it, but he recommended another magician, David Seebach, who came and put on a spectacular magic show.

When a young person is encouraged to reach out and gets a positive response from a figure like the Reverend Billy Graham or David Copperfield, it's amazing what it does for their self-esteem, regardless of the outcome.

A strange story came out of that magic show. In the spiritual world, from paganism to Christianity to Buddhism, you will find concepts of evil spirits or devils. It is believed such spirits can be driven out of or "exorcised" from a person, place, or object.

During the magic show, the entertainer came out on stage dressed in a red cape with a traditional-looking pitchfork, wearing a cap with horns on it.

This infuriated the wives of a number of the priests, especially because the next day was Sunday and liturgy was going to be held on the same stage. The wives felt this guy's "magic" had somehow affected the sanctity of the stage.

After the show, the wives convinced their spouses to perform a series of prayers on the stage, as if they were conducting an exorcism.

After the Sunday liturgy, we always had a special brunch with some dignitaries and all the priests, their wives, and certain other guests, sponsored by FDF and hosted by the metropolitan.

I said to His Eminence, "You'll want to ask some of the priests' wives what took place last night after the magic show."

He looked at me and said, "You're setting me up, I'm sure."

I was, but my reply was, "No, not really. Just ask."

He asked. One of the wives boldly answered with a great deal of pride. She explained what happened, describing the exorcism on stage.

"Oh my God! You didn't," the metropolitan said.

"Yes, we did!" was the reply.

The metropolitan started laughing almost uncontrollably. Afterward, he apologized to the women and did not criticize them, but simply asked why no one came to him to get his take on the matter. I would love to know how he might have reacted.

Perhaps the greatest reward my family and I got out of the years we were involved with FDF was watching young people work to achieve things they never dreamed they could do.

FDF SHOWCASES OTHER CULTURES

One year, a priest from an Alaskan parish described a village in the remote, northernmost region of Alaska that practiced Orthodoxy. They had been converted by a Russian monk who translated the Bible into their native language. The people in the village performed a folk dance that told the story of their conversion.

Hearing that, I was determined to bring the village's dancers to perform at the FDF opening ceremonies.

My plan required the help of a number of people who were well positioned to lend their influence and support. A senior executive at Alaska Airlines went to bat for us and the airline reduced the fare per person by 50 percent. That generous gift made it possible for us to raise the balance of the funds to get them to FDF.

The next big hurdle was coordinating with the Russian diocese in Alaska and the village priest. God was working miracles because 130 men, women, and children (including some infants) left their village for the first time and came to Ontario, California. They performed at FDF, putting on a spectacular and spellbinding performance, dressed in native clothing. One of the villagers narrated what the dance was about and the story of their conversion.

I didn't tell the metropolitan about the villagers in advance. After the performance, he came over, shaking his head and saying, "You never cease to amaze me."

The audience generously applauded and warmly reached out during the weekend. We treated the Alaskan dancers to trips to Disneyland, Universal Studios, and Sea World before they returned home. And to think up to that time none of them had ever left their village.

The parting words from their parish priest was that we had no idea how much we had profoundly changed their lives.

As FDF evolved, we included more people worldwide. If non-US groups didn't want to come and compete, they were still welcome to experience what our kids were experiencing. If they could come to see what was happening, it might inspire them to revive folk dancing in their own countries.

Over the years, we had teams come from Brazil, Argentina, Chile, Paraguay, Honduras, Canada, Bulgaria, Greece, Cyprus, Crete, and Australia—all of whom performed in the US.

Watching those kids come together, becoming friends and dancing together, was a marvelous feeling of accomplishment. The connectivity was powerful and remains so to this day. Holding hands in dance means we are not only in touch with the friend whose hand we hold, but with that friend's parents, grandparents, and great-grandparents, all the way back to Alexander the Great and beyond. Talk about an unbroken connection. How powerful to be able to say that your soul, your spirit, and your emotions reach back to antiquity.

THE YOUTH CONFERENCE

FDF is a program that's sponsored by the church. That was one of the underlying criteria when I created it. This was my promise to Bishop Meletios, whom I went to for permission to start FDF. I believed it was good for the church, and I also believed if it was going to succeed, it had to have the support of the church.

Greek communities are centered around the church, and if the church was to sponsor a cultural event such as FDF and call on its priests to support such a program, we also needed to develop a companion program.

I had made another promise to Bishop Meletios that after the first year we would work on implementing a more religious, education-oriented program as a complementary component of FDF. With the assistance of Father Sam Poulos, of blessed memory, we planned a youth conference that would take place in the fall of the year. Those originally called on to manage the program were FDF dancers Jeff Contos, the Paterakis sisters, Kim Kessaris, George Efstathiou, and Gary Wallner, all from the Northern Conference.

In the second year of FDF, the program known as The Greek Orthodox Youth Conference was launched in Northern California. Any misgivings about holding a religious retreat that would be popular were put to rest. The event surpassed our wildest expectations.

We created a youth conference in which our priests gave educational programs for young people to explore the faith and ask questions. When we officially introduced the youth conference, 250 kids showed up. This showed there was a demand for a new educational program like this. Eventually, one thousand kids were attending the annual youth conference.

As these programs grew, the clergy began to put pressure on the metropolitan, telling him they were too big and should be split, north and south. I was baffled and thought some who had made the program too complex to manage were simply too lazy to continue it.

I had told Metropolitan Anthony if the conference and FDF were split, I wouldn't be a part of it. At that year's youth conference at the Sheraton in Anaheim, the metropolitan called me up to his suite.

"I have good news and bad news," he said.

"Okay. Give me the bad news first and we can talk about the good news later."

He said, "I've made a decision. We're going to split the youth conference, north and south."

"That's a bad decision," I replied. "You will destroy it."

"I've made the decision. We're going to do that, but I'm not touching FDF."

"Okay," was my reply. "I want nothing to do with the youth conference program anymore. I'm out."

Several months went by before I got a call from the metropolitan. I met him at the Metropolis in San Francisco, where he appealed to me to please take charge of the conference to be held in the south.

I agreed but asked him to trust me to do the right thing and give me carte blanche for organizing and running the event. His Eminence was the impatient type and insisted on knowing what I had in mind. I stuck to my guns and asked him to promise to attend. There would be nothing done to embarrass him or the church. He would witness an outstanding program with the potential to change the way programs of this type would be organized in the future.

I presented the challenge His Eminence had given me to others at St. Spyridon and shared my thoughts on how the program might look. I approached a former FDF executive director, Stephanie Angeles, of blessed memory, about taking on the senior management role of the conference. Stephanie worked at the University of California San Diego at the time.

My idea was to take the youth conference away from the hotel environment. I felt hotels set the stage for fun and entertainment—not for serious concentration or as an academic environment. The team liked the idea, and Stephanie convinced the university to rent us some of their facilities that summer, such as classrooms and dorm rooms.

As it turned out, there was one youth conference in the southern territories (Southern California south of Bakersfield, Arizona, Hawaii, and Las Vegas, Nevada) and one in the northern territories (Bakersfield north in Northern California, Oregon, Washington, Alaska, Reno, and Carson City, Nevada), with about 300 kids in each. Stephanie did a marvelous job of coordinating the Southern California conference.

However, that was the last time a youth conference of any consequence was held. A couple attempts were made. One in the south, organized by Evan Arapostathis, seemed to have promise. Despite his amazing effort, the youth conference concept faded away.

An attempt to restart the conference took place in 2021. Held in Long Beach, the event attracted several hundred attendees.

A couple takeaways: One, when contemplating a change, try to project what the unintended consequences of your actions might be. Two, when you change something drastically or stop what you were doing and then try to resurrect it, it's virtually impossible to bring it back. The clergy failed to consider the results of splitting the conference. Unfortunately, no one shed a tear over the program's disappearance, especially the clergy.

FDF CONTINUES TO THRIVE

Fortunately, FDF fared much better than the youth conference. As FDF grew, it began to draw attention internationally in the folk dance community. The folk dance movement continues to grow and thrive in many Greek immigrant communities. The FDF program not only helped preserve a form of folk art and culture, but it also helped ensure future generations' understanding of their heritage.

People were fascinated by what was being created at FDF. They were amazed at how committed our FDF kids were. We often heard comments like:

"How could this possibly be happening? We're in the western US, not Greece."

"This is being done by kids who are second and third generation. They're not closely connected to the motherland and yet they're committed to preserving our culture."

DANCING—AN EMOTIONAL EXPERIENCE

The fact that you can learn to dance something that was danced a hundred years ago, five hundred years ago, one thousand years ago, reawakens the spirit and the soul of perhaps everyone who has danced the dance from the beginning of time.

The idea is that you can listen to music and translate the rhythm into your body. Your body feels that rhythm and applies steps to it, in a unified format, bringing a group of people together.

There is nothing more powerful than people touching one another by holding hands. You may or may not know the person next to you, but the mere fact that you're holding on to each other creates a tremendously emotional feeling, a feeling of unity and a connectivity of spirit.

On top of that, dance mandates that you have a sense of responsibility, coordination, and the ability to perform the steps that the particular dance demands. Perhaps even more important is the connectivity between people that the dance brings. Over the past one hundred years, mankind has experienced a gradual disconnection in which technology has played a major role. The more we become disconnected, the less we see a community. We've seen where we've gone from villages and small cities to large cities where people no longer connect with one another. And now we are creating a world of individuals who only communicate via cell phone. That is, in my opinion, a troublesome situation.

Whenever we Greeks gather as a community, whether for a baptism, a wedding, or a festival of some kind, we always dance. Everyone participates. In all our dances, with few exceptions, it isn't unusual to see an eight-year-old at the head of a line and an eighty-year-old at the end or vice versa. Participation is encouraged; we want the little ones to step in and join the hands of their parents and grandparents. It's a powerful reminder that each of us makes up a chain that unites the whole community.

CAN FOLK DANCE CHANGE THE WORLD?

I don't know if folk dancing can change the world, but I think it can make for more peaceful relationships by building a bridge of community across cultures. The moment you're touching the hand of somebody else, it's almost impossible to hate them or feel any negativity toward them. The energy of the dance can make a big impact when more people participate in it.

Today's modern form of dancing has no connectivity, no teamwork, no sharing the rhythms or emotions. It is disjointed and devoid of human connectivity. It might look nice and entertaining when performed on a stage, but that is where it ends. I recognize that for some, this statement may be disputed, but this is my view and impression of what dance means to me. For instance, in ballroom dancing, holding my partner and dancing is powerful, emotional, and physical. It most definitely demands teamwork and connectivity.

In America and many parts of Western Europe, and perhaps the world, we have lost our understanding of who we are, where we came from, and what our purpose is. One of my dreams was that FDF might inspire other ethnic groups to try to revitalize their ancestral roots.

Is it our purpose in life only to look at a cell phone and text, or is it our purpose to embrace one another, to get to know each other as human beings with souls, emotions, and feelings?

If we separate ourselves with technology, how can we ever get to truly understand what it means to be a human, let alone to sense emotion, pain, joy, and love? Without this human sharing and physical interaction, we risk losing our understanding and our ability to acknowledge our past to better understand our future. Without this we may lose our purpose.

CULTURAL ART FORMS

Part of our goal of preserving our cultural heritage included revitalizing the art form that goes into making costumes and encouraging the mastery of ancient musical instruments.

Greek costumes reflect the geographic regions, from the largest areas to the smallest villages, as well as the influence of other cultures. Here are comments from two of our most knowledgeable FDF dance and costuming judges. The first is from John Lulias of Tarpon Springs, Florida. John is a second-generation Greek American who is dedicated to promoting and preserving Greek culture. He is the recipient of many awards in Greece and the US and is an expert on dances of the Greek islands.

> *Of course, there are a lot of islands in Greece, 2,000, but only a couple hundred that are inhabited. Even dances from various islands are different. The northern Aegean and the Cyclates had some similarities in that they were affected by the cultures of Asia Minor. So, you had these very, very, I want to say delicate steps and lighter dances than you did in the mainland. The costumes themselves were lighter because you're on the islands, so things were brighter and cheerier—the style of island dancing is a much smoother style than I would say of dances from Macedonia or Thrace. Very, very different.*

John Lulias, an expert on Greek dance and culture, and for many years, one of the judges at the Greek Orthodox Folk Dance Festival competition.

George Papangellin from Fresno, California danced at FDF in earliest years, when there were just four communities involved. He went on to become a dance director and continues to judge at the annual competition. He shared these thoughts:

> *The movements tell the story but also folk dancing is just like any other folk art, whether it's Greek folk dancing, or Japanese folk art, or Irish folk attire, or anything else anywhere in the world. It is nature-based. It has to reflect the natural surroundings or*

what natural attributes are available for them to use, whether it's pigments for the colors for dying the yarns and the fabrics or it's the type of yarn. Is it based out of cotton, or is it wool, or is it silk? Those are all natural things.

They didn't have nylons and rayons way back in the day. They had natural products. They had mountains, they had rivers, they had valleys, they had flat lands, they had hilly lands, so they had to work among those physical, those natural surroundings as well. All of that, in addition to the clothing that was worn, based on the time of year and the climate, and how hot is it, or how cold is it, how snowy is it or how dry is it, the colors, and the weight of the fabrics, and the number of layers of clothing that were worn, that all had and has an effect or an impact on movement.

It's a bigger story than what you just see with your eyes, watching movement. There's a whole lot more to it than that, and it takes a long time to get it.

FDF was privileged to tap into the expertise and support of costume experts from Greece and the US, including Anna Efstathiou and Vilma Machette, both of blessed memory. Many of the parents, such as Bertha Angels, Dena Stamos (of blessed memory), Ava Angelopoulos, and Irene Peros (Simvoulakis), shared their experience, conducted in-depth research, and created remarkably authentic-looking costumes for the dancers. The incredible artistry in each costume—the sourcing of appropriate fabrics and trim, the ornate embroidery and meticulous stitching of the costumes, including belts and shoes—was phenomenal.

They also represent the maker's artistry. A costume holds the imprint of who someone is. In the past, the "costume" a woman wore was part of her dowry and was often the dress in which she was married.

When FDF originally wanted to reconnect to that art form, many immigrant grandmothers were still with us. In those early days, you could visit a community and see mothers and grandmothers sewing costumes, passing on the tradition to their children or grandchildren. It seems to still exist, but not to the extent it did in the early years of the movement.

THE ART OF THE DANCE

Many of our dances tell a story. Greek dancing is an art that's integral to Greek history.

The Dance of Zalongo, for example, replicates the actions of a group of Greek women known as the Souliotes, that took place in 1903. Rather than be subjugated by the Turks (Ottomans), they chose to die. Realizing the inevitable, they literally danced off a cliff, falling to their deaths while holding their children in their arms.

It's an emotional and powerful dance that depicts an important moment in history when the Greeks lived under the yoke of the Ottoman Empire. The dance's music comes from the voices of the dancers; no instruments are played, which makes the dance even more poignant and emotional as you hear the last voice fall over the cliff. The story tells us that the only sound was the sound of singing, not screaming, as the women danced off the cliff. I think about that and chills go up my spine.

WHAT I MOST LOVED ABOUT FDF

If I had to pick one favorite thing about FDF, it's that I had the opportunity and privilege to work with young people.

I loved teaching them the business skills that have been taken away from young people today. The kids learned a sense of responsibility, what it takes to make a dollar, and how to commit to an idea and then follow through. In today's society, those types of lessons have been almost eliminated from the lives of many young people. When I was young you could water your neighbor's lawn, deliver papers, or be a box boy or girl at the local grocery store to make extra money. Today, few kids are given those opportunities. In fact, today there are few jobs that can teach "adulting" skills—unless you're a young person raised on a farm or in a rural community. Newspapers are now being delivered by adults.

When I was a paperboy, I learned about business and about being responsible. Starting as a fifteen-year-old box boy, I worked my way up to being a clerk. These are opportunities that don't exist as much today for young people—or perhaps these are opportunities their parents may not consider as important as playing baseball or soccer.

I'm all in favor of team sports because they encourage teamwork and good health. In addition, they impart a sense of community. But beyond that, they do nothing to prepare a person for life and the challenges they will face. In fact, in some respects it has become a negative because at the end of the season every player receives a trophy, regardless of their ability. What is the lesson being taught here? We are, through youth sports, unwittingly debasing the concept of seeking to achieve "excellence."

I remember over the years there was one parent from a city in Arizona, a well-educated professional, who came up to me to ask, "Why must there be competition at FDF?" He said his daughter cried because her team didn't win a medal. My response was always the same: It was the parent's responsibility to point out that if we want to win, we must be committed to the idea of excellence. I would point out that from the day a baby passes through the birth canal they enter a world of perpetual competition—first to survive the journey of being born, then school, then work, then life in general. I told him how amazing it was to me that, with his background as a medical doctor, an OB/GYN specialist in academics, he complained about competition. I suggested he teach his child to be a good loser and come back next year and work harder.

For some reason, many parents now coddle their children and are afraid to let them fail. I wish they understood it's the small missteps in life that strengthen our character and our resolve. Worrying about the possibility of injuring their children's feelings is a serious mistake. At least, that is one man's opinion.

It wasn't always easy to make those choices. In my thirty-five years of being involved with the program, every young person I dealt with was an outstanding individual who you couldn't help but love and respect. And we wanted everyone to work hard in anticipation of being selected to serve on the senior management team. The SMT gave the program continuity from year to year and was our way of keeping the knowledge base intact and transferable. It was the mechanism of passing it forward. I believe that foundation has allowed it to continue to exist. In 2020, the program celebrated its forty-fourth anniversary. I say we did our job well—all of us.

Finally, and perhaps most importantly, is the lesson of being a gracious loser and recognizing maybe you didn't prepare as hard as the winner did. When we remove the value of competition and treat everyone the same, the sense of entitlement sets in. I think of the attitude of those original immigrants who came to the US for a better life. They worked hard and relished the opportunity this nation gave everyone who was not afraid to try and succeed. I wish the same for our children. Why are we afraid of competition when we should embrace it, to let it teach us how to better cope in a world that revolves around competition? How do we change the loser into being a winner? It's amazing to me that such a simple concept is so badly distorted. It is in the trying that we become winners, not whether we actually win. It is a process that expands our abilities and horizons and turns us into possibility thinkers and doers.

We worked on replicating this program in the southern US with what eventually became known as the Hellenic Folk Dance Festival. I believe if not for Sandy Papadopoulos and Gerry Clonaris, Archon of the Ecumenical Patriarchate of the Greek Orthodox Church, we might not have had the courage to try. They launched a winning program.

To say we got it started would be unfair to those in the South who worked so hard to convince their metropolitan the idea was worth exploring. They got it off the ground and it was tracking almost exactly like ours, growing at the same rate. However, the adults who controlled the program began to question the necessity of competition and eventually removed it from the festival. The only awards were things like Honorable Mention. In time, the festival once again became a competition with awards for teams finishing in the top three places.

The attitude of the children who had lost the ability to compete was: Why go every week and rehearse and rehearse and rehearse to get an Honorable Mention or share the same award with another team? It seems the adults were afraid they might injure the children's sensibilities or emotions. But kids are strong and resilient. It is in their nature, as well as mankind's nature, to compete. Strip the sense of achieving without a carrot at the other end and you will create a generation of incompetent and entitled thinkers. Therein lies the seed of a nation's decline. It can be called "embedded laziness."

Trying to insulate children from competition only weakens them for the future. The program in the South should have grown in size equal to FDF, if not larger, but there have been no signs of that being achieved. The program still exists, but it has tried to do too many things besides dance and a choral group competition. I see that with FDF today; they are trying to introduce too many other programs that take away from the core aspect of FDF, when doing so demonstrates a lack of imagination, creativity, and vision. If there is a need for these other programs, develop them on their own; don't tie them to a successful program, for you risk dragging the successful program down. In the South, we see the formation of a program called ANOIXI, where young people come to just learn dance and enjoy fellowship with certain outside influences.

Koinonia is a similar group in Los Angeles. Their formation is in essence a protest of what has been taken away; they are seeking to replace the void they perceive.

I'm immensely proud of our FDF kids. They learned an amazing number of dances, from regions as diverse as Crete, Pontos, Asia Minor, northern Greece, and southern Greece, as well as the islands. The kids do these dances with ease. They hear the music and they're into the dance. I marvel at what they can do and have accomplished.

In essence, the kids brought the dances back to life. Without the stimulus of competition, would the level and quality of dance have reached the level of sophistication it has? The pursuit of excellence is a powerful and dynamic force, and it should be encouraged at all times in everything we attempt to do. It is interesting that the national church sponsors an oratorical competition in all the metropolises, and the winner of each age group goes to the national competition. They are able to choose from a series of religious topics to develop their presentation. It seems the various parishes embrace this form of competition. Why is that?

Is it that it makes the church feel comfortable that our youth are giving a speech about some aspect of the faith? The intent is good, but how many people does it reach and to what extent does it make the church more real and necessary in their lives? Yes, it may help the clergy feel good. But feeling good and having an impact are not the same.

The question is: Do you want to strengthen the faith you have, to build a commitment as a warrior, like Saint Paul? If not for Saint Paul, I am not sure Christianity would have developed the deep roots needed to withstand the test of time.

Over the years, I have been asked about the inspiration for FDF. My experiences at the Rose Bowl and the Church of Latter-day Saints planted the seeds, but it actually was another series of occurrences that helped formulate the concept for FDF.

As the youth director at St. Spyridon, I was introduced to some amazing and talented young adults, many of whom were involved in Greek dance. For those involved in the dance, it was not only an extra-curricular activity from their studies and part-time work, but also a passion. It was inspiring to observe someone working hard at a craft without being paid and only being motivated by wanting to learn and to perfect their efforts in learning the dances.

Our young adults wanted an opportunity to show what they had achieved, and approached me, asking to be part of the entertainment at the church's annual food festival. I saw no reason why they shouldn't. At that point it became a question of convincing the adults in leadership positions at the church and those on the St. Spyridon Annual Food Festival committee that it was a good idea. The rest is history.

I remember telling the FDF kids about the Rose Bowl experience and how I thought Greek dance could be just as big. They thought I was joking, but I believe in shooting for the moon, which is how I've lived my whole life. Again, I think this speaks to our failure of not inspiring young kids. America is the only place in the world where you can do whatever you want and be as successful as you want if you're committed to it.

As FDF grew, I think the kids all began to believe we could grow to be as large as the dance event my wife and I witnessed at the Rose Bowl. Frankly, they did make it happen.

When I was involved with FDF, the age of dancers ranged from five to senior citizens. On a few occasions, we had dance groups of people in their fifties, sixties, and seventies. Today, I don't see enough of the older generation willing to get up on stage and perform. We had created a special No Compete division, hoping to attract the older generation who want to come for the joy of being involved. These dancers were there not to compete, but to demonstrate the beauty of the generational attributes of the dance.

If I am disappointed with how the FDF operation is run today, it's that we've restricted the leadership to people in their twenties. When I was in charge, we had members of the management team as young as fourteen. I think eliminating the younger kids is a tragedy because the adults, while well meaning, have lost the essence of the founding principles of FDF.

The truth is, managing twenty young kids from ages thirteen to twenty-one is not an easy job. It's a commitment, and if you're not committed to working with that diversity of age groups, you shouldn't take on this job. My passion was to impart whatever I could to that group, to try to replace what modern society has taken away from them, and to help them develop the ability to be possibility thinkers, so anything they set their mind to, they could do—given the time and commitment to achieve.

It also allowed the older members to learn to be mentors to the younger ones and teach a great lesson of charity and outreach. For me it was a way to pay it forward in memory of Doc Mosby.

In many ways the program was successful. But did it achieve my ultimate dream? No. Like so many things, we sometimes try to do too much or find we don't have the resources or the commitment from enough individuals willing to step up to the plate. Since the basic program we had created and implemented was working, many thought there was no need to elevate it to the next level.

Perhaps the greatest reward I could say my family and I got out of the years I was involved with FDF was watching young people working to achieve things they never dreamed they could do.

Shaping The Individual

My love for dance started in fifth grade. My teacher was Ms. Wilson, a stout woman with bright red hair and freckles. Unmarried, she traveled the world every summer and had a passion for folk dance. Part of her yearly curriculum was folk dance.

I already mentioned I was part of a square dance group at the University of Arizona. To earn extra money, I worked for the Tucson Park and Recreation Department, coaching little league and Pop Warner teams for $1.50 per hour.

My coaching style was not trying to create championship teams, but to teach the sport and the nuances of the game. It was my goal to give each child an experience at every position on the team.

An example is one of my Pop Warner teams. Little Johnny was a chubby kid who wasn't the most coordinated athlete. I wanted him to get a sense of what it was like to be the quarterback. Through coaxing and workouts, he got his chance. Part of the coaching was getting the other team members to recognize that we were there to learn and help one another. With the support of his teammates, Johnny got the experience of knowing and understanding what it was like to be the quarterback. His teammates never criticized him; only praised and congratulated him. Johnny went back to his position on the line. Every kid on the team had the same opportunity to see what it was like.

I probably still have the record for the most complaint letters written by parents, but my biggest fan club was made up of kids. They got it. All my teams won some games, but what we learned and experienced was invaluable. Today, Johnny can say with pride that he once was a quarterback at a big school, knowing in his heart what it means to be part of a team.

LOOKING FORWARD

The FDF program of today is as dynamic as ever from a dance competition perspective. From the outside looking in, it has significantly advanced technologically, with live streaming of the activities. The idea that these performances could now be shared around the world is magnificent.

The program has been able to obtain financial sponsors at a significant level to help underwrite the costs associated with it.

People gather from all over the western US and offer a platform to continue, maintain, and support the history of the Hellenes.

One caution: If you want to create your own FDF, don't try to turn it into something it isn't by adding too many religious and/or educational components. Too often, one wants to take the easy path, when achieving a goal requires discipline and determination. Try to simply tack things on to a successful event and you begin to weaken the entire program. Start with your moonshot clearly defined and in place as your goal. Begin by taking baby steps, with each step getting bigger as start to achieve incremental success.

CHAPTER 14

The Family And FDF

"I loved the FDF program, from dancing to the administrative side to being a spectator in the crowd. I created new friends and saw old friends; it was like one big, happy family."

NICHOLAS JOHN PREOVOLOS, PETER AND LITSA'S SON

FDF CAME AT a time when I was also launching a brand-new business. I've often wondered whether our business would have grown a lot faster if FDF hadn't come into my life.

On the other hand, would my business have survived had it not been for FDF? Because with FDF, I believed we were doing God's work.

We are doing God's work any time we are helping our fellow man. FDF was a unique outreach program benefiting a lot of people for a lot of different reasons. For many people, it gave them a purpose, and for others it created a new life, a new outlet to express themselves. For still others, it revitalized their spirit and perhaps their beliefs. For some, it has reawakened the spirit of their ancestors.

My family members were the foundation and the support that enabled the building of FDF. They were the backbone. Never once did they challenge the craziness of taking on such a project. Of course, when it started, my kids were still in grammar school.

My wife, Litsa, stepped up to the plate and supported me and all of the FDF activities. She, along with Don and Ellie Hiatt, ran the "back office," making FDF work and everything succeed, from helping to publish the FDF newspaper, *Oli Mazi*, to entering the judges' scores for each dance and supervising the judges. They acted as my sounding board, made solid decisions, and offered some of the best and most innovative management and creative ideas.

In the early days, all the scores were done by hand. Don, Ellie, and Litsa hand-calculated the scores, and then totaled them to determine where each team placed. Usually, they stayed up performing calculations until the wee hours of the morning, tabulating the scores that were necessary for the next day's round of competition.

Mark Morenz, a computer consultant who worked with our company, Alpha & Omega, eventually developed a computerized program with the help of my wife, Don, Ellie, and my son Nicholas. It was FDF's first computerized scoring program. Mark volunteered his services for years, and we are deeply grateful to him for his generosity.

Litsa alone was responsible for inputting the scores for thirty-five years. We once estimated she had entered at least a million digits per each FDF and each was flawless. She's absolutely amazing.

As far as my family and my business were concerned, FDF took over for several months of the year.

There was a time every year when, if you walked into our office and asked our staff, "Who do you work for?" the answer you might hear was, "I think we're working for FDF."

We called on our staff to do a lot of support work, whether it was mailings or something else. In fact, we even took them up to FDF to help the management team with behind-the-scenes jobs at our expense. Not only did our family put our heart and soul into this project, so did many of our employees. Financially, we did our part as well.

All three of my sons started out dancing with their respective age groups by being part of a dance program at St. Spyridon, as well as performing. As they got older, in high school and college, each of them joined the management team and had a shot at being the managing director of FDF. Of course, that meant they had to put up with people who thought they were selected because they were my kids. I'd like to think that wasn't the sole criteria and we selected them because we believed they could perform properly and had the passion for the program, and, above all, they had earned the right to be considered for the position.

CHAPTER 15

The Future

"It always seems impossible until it is done."
NELSON MANDELA

THIS BOOK ATTEMPTS to highlight the various events that helped sculpt the person I have become today. Besides my mother, who gave birth to me and raised me, my wife, Litsa, has been my rock.

Litsa has been the architect of who I am as a man, husband, father, and business owner. Throughout our fifty years of marriage, she has been my best critic and champion. Her task, given my personality, wasn't always an easy one. I hated it when she pointed out my shortcomings and failings or when she had to remind me to do something, but that was the honing process that contributed to who I am today. I still have a long way to go. If nothing else, Litsa has earned the right to be canonized.

My father has my eternal gratitude for instilling in me my character and giving me the roadmap of how I should live my life. He respected everyone, regardless of color, race, religion, or political opinion. He always showed the highest respect for his fellow man, and I never heard him criticize anyone or any group.

Dad admired his contemporaries, such as Albert Schweitzer and Mahatma Gandhi.

When the restaurant closed during the Depression, my dad was determined to repay everyone who was owed money. Some called him foolish for caring, but he cared, and although it took twenty years, he paid everyone back.

I admired him, his ways, and his ethics, so much so that I have always said if I could achieve one-fourth of what he was in his life, I would consider myself a very successful man. All I can tell my father is that I tried, it was hard, and sometimes I stumbled. But I would like to think he would be proud of what I have done and what I have achieved. When I stumbled, it was through God's grace and my family's love and tolerance that I managed to right myself and get back into balance. Thank God I didn't get off track too often.

My father-in-law, Thomas Poulos, was another extraordinary example of tenacity and determination. He came to America as a stowaway aboard a ship at the age of twelve. He went on to own and operate a small chain of theaters in Colorado. His life was also an inspiration and an example that anything is possible (please see Appendix A for the eulogy given at his funeral).

Questions about the accuracy of my story: Memories are personal recollections that tend to morph over time. Wherever possible, my editors have attempted to check the accuracy of objective facts, names, and dates.

As I stated at the beginning of this journey, stories are often founded in oral traditions and histories passed down from one generation to the next. They are often embellished and modified. Does that make a story less correct, wrong, or bad? Every time the story is told it is told in the context of the moment, the current period of history and cultural environment and social experience of the storyteller.

To understand our own stories, it is critical for each of us to have a sense of who we are and where we have come from, as well as awareness of the challenges and accomplishments of our immediate family and ancestors.

Of equal importance is knowing how and why our great nation of the US was formed. Consider the sacrifices made by our founders, plus their cooperation and brilliance in writing the Declaration of Independence, the Constitution, and the Bill of Rights. If we fail to try to understand this, as a nation we become rudderless and lose our direction.

As Americans, our freedoms are at risk:

- The opportunity to live and work in an environment that allows us to be as productive and creative as we want

- To be able to speak our minds and express ourselves without fear of retribution of any kind

- To practice our own belief system, as long as it does not infringe on someone else's rights or freedoms

My fear today is that our political leadership has polarized many segments of society; we have handcuffed expression of speech by creating something called political correctness. We are moving to the fringes of both the right and the left.

It frightens me to think that Americans, who represent roughly 6 percent of the world's population, are the only nation on this planet to enjoy this incredible freedom. Maintaining it demands a well-educated public that understands the importance of knowledge and participation in the process, and what it means to be a fiduciary of the greatest document ever conceived by man, the US Constitution.

HAVE WE LOST OUR RUDDER?

The beliefs of my parents and my culture were the seeds that made me who I became as an adult. But many of the concepts I learned seem to be disappearing today. My family and culture emphasized a strong work ethic, our religion, and political awareness. Today, we seem to be bombarded by media that focuses on the negative elements of what is going on in society. From my perspective, the media continues to choose sensationalism and negativism, rather than building up society with the positive news about the world's accomplishments. Yet they have a fiduciary responsibility to society to balance the good with the bad, and to guard against interjecting their biases. They fail to embrace being stewards to society and keeping world events in balance, with objectivity.

We've done a poor job of educating people, especially when it comes to the founding principles of America. The people who signed the Constitution and the Declaration of Independence were an incredible group of human beings from various walks and experiences of life. They were universally educated in the arts, philosophy, history, business, economics, and law. They had a vast array of knowledge and a broad vision. They could call on the great philosophers of Greece and Rome, the great artists and artisans, scientists, and world history itself to access an idea or issue. They were critical thinkers who could objectively evaluate the issues they faced. Because of their backgrounds and broad education, they had the tools to dissect issues and evaluate the truth.

Today, no one, certainly no one in politics, offers that inspiration or that vision of true leadership. We have become what one might describe as a rudderless society. Remove the lessons of our Founding Fathers or the commentary found within the Federalist Papers, and you've stripped all sense of direction and purpose. Today, many educators specialize in indoctrination rather than education.

We seem to have stepped back from educating people, so they have the ability to think and use tools to access all aspects of an issue. It starts with our kids, but even as adults, we should never stop trying to learn and develop.

MY FAITH IN GOD

Whatever I may have achieved or accomplished in my life's journey wouldn't have been possible without my commitment and belief in God. I have come to the belief that each time I fall, God is there to help me rise up to rebuild a stronger foundation that takes me to the next level.

I believe challenges, both positive and negative, are God's way of testing and preparing us for what is to come. With each step, the seed of faith is planted and nurtured. I am beginning to understand that God's rightness is secured only by faith, not works.

Saint Paul wrote: "But we also glory in tribulation, knowing that tribulation produces perseverance, and perseverance character, and character hope."

The trials, difficulties, and adversities are, in my opinion, God's way of preparing us to try and achieve *theosis*.[2] It is by faith that we can overcome and develop a better understanding of how God uses adversity in molding our character and strengthening our resolve to persevere.

Throughout trials and adversities, patience combined with faith has allowed me to overcome the challenges.

In closing this chapter of my story, I offer these words for consideration.

- Never abandon God. Put your faith in Him.

- When you set out to do something, shoot for the moon and do not let roadblocks get in your way. Ignore thoughts like, "it can't be done, it's impossible; don't waste your time, it's too hard; it's going to take too long" and move ahead!

- When you start out to do something, invoke God's help, and when you feel you are at a point of desperation, call on God and tell Him you can't do this without His help. Then keep moving forward.

- Expect to surprise yourself one day as you lift up your head to see that you have not only reached your goal but exceeded it.

May God's blessing be ever present in your life. May your faith always shine brightly in your personal journey and especially during those moments when things seem hopeless. Do not give up, for God will guide you through those minefields—and remember, He never gives up on you.

Try God. It works. It certainly has for me.

A. Acknowledgments

THERE ARE SO many people who influenced my life that it would be difficult to express my gratitude to them all in only a page or two. Nevertheless, it is important to name a few.

I thank my parents, Nicholas and Fofo, for giving me a passion for reading and discovery. A lot of my thoughts and creative side were molded by both of them. My mother stimulated my creative side while my father instilled in me my philosophy, ethics, and respect for mankind. I learned by watching their actions and at the dinner table, where we were encouraged to express our views and think about and discuss events of the day and our experiences.

My maternal step-grandmother, Mabel Touloumis, played a major role in introducing me to the value of being a stamp collector (philatelist) and someone who can appreciate movies; she deserves praise for sharing her passion for these things with me when I was very young.

I have always admired Doc Mosby, my DeMolay chapter advisor and mentor, for teaching me to be a possibility thinker. His ability convinced me, as a fourteen-year-old boy, that I could go to the most prestigious hotel in San Francisco and negotiate a contract to hold a dance. This showed me that anything is possible if you're willing to invest the time and effort.

My heartfelt gratitude goes to my wife, Litsa, and sons, Thanasi, Nicholas, and Spiro, for their support and encouragement to write this book.

I am indebted to my cousin Louis "Troy" Preovolos, of blessed memory, for allowing us into his home to be interviewed for the purpose of getting a better picture of the family history. Louis, now in his nineties, is our oldest living relative in America.

I value author Nancy Hendrickson for the hours she spent with me, asking questions, and not only recording all our conversations, but also transcribing the recordings. Nancy organized the text into an order that gave this book a sense of sequence, purpose, and meaning.

In the last eight years, writer/director Patti Testerman has worked as a partner, cheerleader, and an inspiration in helping me complete three major projects. The first was the creation of a unique cultural website called "A Web of Culture." The second was telling the story of the Greek Orthodox Folk Dance and Choral Festival in an award-winning documentary called "Kefi." The third is this book, which I started at the same time I began to develop the family tree, when I was fifteen years old.

Patti's patience and ability to handle difficult experiences included navigating diverse opinions and biases. Her perseverance outpaced my own determination to complete these projects. Her positive perspective and love for her work uplifted and reassured me that the projects were important, not only to me but to the community. I shall be eternally grateful.

Finally, many thanks go to my copy editor, Beth Mansbridge, who tells me she enjoyed this assignment of polishing the manuscript, and that my life story is fascinating to read. Beth certainly knew how to get to my ego.

With all my love, respect, and admiration,

Dad, grandfather, mentor, businessman, senior citizen, and friend, especially to the community of FDF

B. About The Author

PETER E. PREOVOLOS speaks on the twelve life lessons on how to live life to the fullest. He has enjoyed a long and very successful career in the employee benefits industry. It began at Wells Fargo Bank, where he opened the Employee and Asset Management Division for Southern California operations. In 1974, he joined Southern California First National Bank as Vice President in charge of statewide employee benefit services. In 1979, he left the banking industry and became CEO of Alpha & Omega Financial Management Consulting Inc, a third-party administration (TPA) and asset management firm. In 1994, he and twenty other TPAs joined forces in forming PenChecks, Inc. where he was elected president of the PenChecks family of companies. An acknowledged leader in the pension benefits distribution field, Peter holds professional designations as a Registered Investment Advisor (RIA) and an Accredited Pension Administrator (APA). He is one of approximately three hundred people in the United States to earn the prestigious credential of Accredited Investment Fiduciary Analyst (AIFA). If you would like a conversation about having Peter speak to your group, please send an email to emanuelfotini@gmail.com.

C. Notes

1 Lee Moriwaki. "The Rev. Homer Demopulos, Highly Respected Seattle Priest." *Seattle Times,* May 29, 1993.
2 As previously mentioned in the manuscript, *theosis* is a Greek word for a transformative process whose aim is likeness to or union with God, as taught by the Eastern Orthodox Church and the Byzantine Catholic Churches.

D. Index

Abbott and Costello, 52

accounting error, 75

actuaries, 93–95

Adams, Nicky, 107

ADP, 97

Adventurer of the Nineteenth Century, 105

Aegean Dancers, 107–108, 118–119

aerospace consultant, 115

Agamemnon, 4

Alaskan dancers, 127

Alexander the Great, 3, 32, 128

Alexander, "King of the Hellenes", 10

allergy, 30

Alpha & Omega, v, 76, 78, 80–81, 86, 90, 97, 144

America, ii, v, 7–11, 20–21, 25, 29, 34–35, 58, 132, 140, 148, 150

American Society of Pension Professionals & Actuaries, 93

American Tobacco Company, 82

Americans, 30, 40, 108, 149

ancestors, viii, 3, 121, 143, 148

Angeles-Thomas, Connie, 107

Angelopoulos, Ava, 134

Angels, Bertha, 134

Annenberg, Joyce, 97

Annunciation Cathedral, Oakland, CA, 69

ANOIXI, 138

Antigone, 3

antiquity, 48, 105, 128

Arbuckle, Ernest C. "Ernie", 71

Arcadia, 4

Arestis, George, 14

Arkansas, 35

Ascension Cathedral, Oakland, CA, 108, 113

Asia Minor, 118–119, 133, 138

Asimidis, 20–21

ASPPA, 93

asthma, 29, 37, 58

Athan, Nick, 107

Athanasios, 8, 68

Atherton Country Club, 53

Aunt Bessie, 16–17

Auto Rollover Default IRA, 99

awards, 133, 137

Bakersfield, 70, 130

Balkan Wars, 7

Bank of San Diego, 77, 86–87, 90–91

bank regulations, 73

Banks, 70, 75, 86–87, 89, 93–95, 99

Basdakis, John, 107

Basdakis, Zino, 107

Beal Jr., Carlton, 53

Beal, Barry, 53

Bechtel Corporation, 100

benefit consultants, 93

benefit payment processing, 96

best business practices, 109–110

Bill of Rights, 149

Black Jack Jerome, 17

Blair, Tony, 7

board of directors, 85, 102–103

boot camp, 9

boxer, 40

Boyle, Jim, 85, 90

brother Ted, 24, 34, 36

Brown, F. Seth, 71, 73–74

Bruckner, Alex, 90

budget, 45, 77, 95, 97, 111–113, 116, 124–125

Bulgaria, 110, 127

Buscos, Mike, 52

business plan, 77

business school, 52

California, viii, 8, 14, 17, 22, 35, 37–38, 43, 46, 68–71, 73, 75, 78, 83, 85–87, 89, 91, 95, 98, 112, 114, 125, 127–130, 133

California Chapter of the, 43

Callahan, Michael, 97

Camp Lewis, Washington, 10

Camus, Albert, 19

Cannery, 64

Cantos, Roxanne, 107

Carolan, Robert, 97

Carter, Jimmy, 86

Catalogue of Ships, 4

Catholic and Jewish charities, 45

CBS Sports, 80–81

Cedars-Sinai Medical Center, 69

Cherokee North American Indians, 22

chewing tobacco, 39

Chicago, 8

childhood, v, 29–31, 33, 35, 37, 39, 41, 49, 54

children, viii, 2–3, 8, 17, 19–23, 35, 39, 44, 48, 62, 79, 115–117, 123, 127, 134–138

chores, 35, 38–39

Christenson, C. James, 97

Christenson, Jim, 95

church festival, 106–107

Church of Latter-day Saints, 139

cigar, 14, 22, 25, 36, 39

classes, 14, 106–107

college, v, 10, 30, 37–38, 49, 51–55, 57, 59, 62–63, 77, 114, 144

commission, 25–26, 73–74

communication, 52, 103, 114

community, 3, 15–16, 30–31, 55, 70–71, 82, 94, 102, 106–108, 110–113, 116, 123, 128, 130–136

competition, 88, 107, 109, 117–122, 124, 133, 136–139, 142, 144

confidence, v, 43, 45, 47, 49, 114

Congress, ii, 10, 94, 99

Connecticut, 82

Constantine, James, 20–21

Constitution, 149–150

Continental Grain, 58

Contos, Jeff, 128

Cooley, Richard P. "Dick", 71
Copperfield, David, 125
Corcovado, 20–21
Cordova, Sal, 63
costumes, 107–108, 117, 120–121, 133–134
costuming judges, 133
courage, 69, 76, 137
Covey, Stephen, 95, 112
COVID pandemic, 98, 108
Crete, 7, 106, 127, 138
cultural background, 32
cultural heritage, 133
cultural preservation, 116
culture, 3, 60, 105, 114, 120–121, 130–131, 133, 149
cultures, 3, 32, 126, 132–133
Cyprus, 7, 127
dance, 44–47, 55, 61, 105–111, 117–124, 126–127, 130–133, 135, 137–142, 144
Daughters of the American Revolution, 44
Declaration of Independence, 148, 150
Default Auto Rollover bill, 99
defined benefit pension and cash balance plans, 94
Del Monte, 64–65, 67
DeMolay, 43–47, 53
DeNaronia, Senorita, 58
Department of Labor, 94, 99
Depression, 16, 29, 35, 148
Douglas, Lewis Williams, 10
Drosky, Tom, 98
Efstathiou, Anna, 134

Efstathiou, George, 128
Ehrmans, 70
Ellis Island, 20–21
emphysema, 58
Employee Retirement Income Security Act, 90
employees, viii, 45, 71, 87, 94, 97, 102, 144
English, 7, 9, 23, 60
Epirus, 106
Erasmia, 19–21
ERISA, 90, 98, 100
ethics, 19, 24, 30, 35, 110, 148, 157
Euclid, 3
Fahouris, George, 107
Fairmont Hotel, 46–47, 72
fairness, 60
family, v, vii, 3–5, 7–9, 11, 15–17, 19–23, 25–26, 30, 32, 34–37, 44, 54, 58, 62, 68, 70, 74, 106, 126, 141, 143–145, 148–149
farm, 8, 11, 15, 35–41, 135
Farmer & Ridley LLP, 98
father, viii–1, 4–5, 8–9, 13–14, 19–23, 26, 30–32, 34–35, 40, 52, 54, 58–60, 68, 116–117, 122–123, 128, 147–148, 150, 157
FDF, v, 106–130, 132–136, 138–145
FDIC-insured investments, 98
Ferrari, 54
Festival Dancers, 108
fiduciary, 100–101, 103, 149
financial analyst, 114
find ratio, 101

First National Bank, 71

Flamson, Richard J., 85

Florida, 7, 82, 133

Fofo, 16–17, 19–21, 23

folk dance community, 110, 130

folk dancing, 109–111, 114, 121–122, 127, 132–133

food festival, 106–107, 139

Foodmaker, Inc., 72

football, 43, 51–53, 67

Ford, President Gerald, 100

Frangotis, Minnie, 36

Gallanis, Patricia, 107

Gallanis, Themis, 107

gambling, 78, 81–82

Gandhi, Mahatma, 59, 147

Ganohora, Turkey, 20

Garies, Betty and Jerry, 106

Glaser Brothers, 25–26

Glendale, 56, 70

GOLD (Greek Orthodox Leadership Development), 111–112

gold miners, 15

Golden Gate Avenue, 15

Golden Gate Bridge, 53

Good Friday, 33

Gotses, Christine, 107

grandchildren, viii, 134

grandmother, 19, 21, 134

Great Depression, 16, 29

Greece, 4, 7–9, 15, 20–21, 32, 35, 44, 58, 106–108, 110, 118–121, 127, 131, 133–134, 138, 150

Greek American, 133

Greek Bazaar, 108

Greek Business Guide and Directory, 15

Greek culture, 105, 133

Greek Dance, 105–106, 108, 110, 117–120, 123, 133, 139

Greek dance, 105–106, 108, 110, 117–120, 123, 133, 139

Greek folk dancers, 110

Greek folk dancing, 109, 133

Greek heritage, 19, 30, 77

Greek independence, 118–119

Greek Orthodox, vii, 26–27, 32–33, 35, 45, 69, 106–108, 111, 114, 122, 128, 133, 137

Greek War of Independence, 4

Greeks, 3, 7–8, 15, 20–21, 32, 60, 131, 135

Hackett, Buddy, 82

Halinnan, James, 97

Halleck, Lowell, 77, 87, 90

Hancock, John, 102

Hasapiko, 109

Hell's Kitchen Bill-Bill, 24

Hellenes, 3, 10, 110, 142

Heller Ehrman, 70

Heslin, Father Patrick, 14

Hialeah Park Racetrack, 82

Hibernia Bank, 15

honesty, 60

hospital, 29–30, 36, 59

immigrant, 25, 34, 60, 130, 134

immigrants, 3, 15–16, 30, 34, 137

Imperial Grill, 8–9, 11, 13–14, 16–17, 23–25

Imperial Theater, 13
influenza epidemic, 21
Inglewood, 21
Innocenti, Ray, 87
inspiration, 48, 65, 139, 148, 150
insurance companies, 93, 95
International Brotherhood of
    Teamsters, 63
International Foundation of
    Employee Benefit Plans, 98
International Order of DeMolay, 43
investments, 94, 98
investors, 97
Irish folk attire, 133
IRS, 93–95, 100
Istanbul, 19
Ives, Burl, 43
job, v, 33, 35, 44, 46–47, 53, 58–59,
    61–65, 67, 69, 72–73, 77, 80, 89,
    113–114, 124, 130, 135, 137, 140,
    144, 150
Job's Daughters, 44, 46–47
Johnson, Charles E., 97
Jones Street, 15
Judging, 121–122
July, 29
Junior Parish Council, 106
Kalamatiano, 109, 117
Kaliope, 17
Katina, 34
Kennedy, President John F., 56
Kentucky Derby, 81
Kessaris, Kim, 128
Kessner, Cheri, 97

King of Mycenae, 4
Koinonia, 138
Kokas, Andrew, 16, 23, 36
Kolokotronis, Theodoros, 4
Kotsiomitis Stamison, Amy, 113
Kreder, James G., 97
Kromydas, Marilyn, 107
Kumeloswa, Leo, 43
Lake Tahoe, 47
Las Vegas, 79, 81–82, 130
Latter-day Saints, Church of, 108, 139
law school, 38, 67
Le Havre, France, 8
leadership, 43, 45, 88, 111–117, 139–140,
    149–150
Leadership Program, 111
legacy, 16
Libby's Candy, 20–21
Libby's canned goods, 21
liquor, 17, 26, 31
Litsa, 41, 64, 68, 76, 80, 114, 143–144,
    147
Livingston Bros., 16
Lodi, 35–36
Los Angeles, 20–21, 63, 68–71, 78, 85,
    88, 90, 98, 106, 108, 124, 138
Lowell High School, 51
Lulias, John, 133
Macedonia, 133
Machette, Vilma, 134
Magers, Geraldine "Gerrie", 112
Man Mountain Dean, 24

management team, 78, 103, 111, 124, 136, 140, 144

managing director, FDF, 144

Market Street, 9, 13–14

marriage, 2, 4, 16, 21–23, 27, 37, 41, 68, 147

Mary the Theotokos, 27

Masonic Order, 43–44

Masons and Shriners, 43

Mayo Clinic, 30

Mays, Willie, 62

McAllister Street, 13

McCoy, Rita, 86

media, 149

medicine, 59

Meletios, Bishop, 128

Menlo College, 51–53

Mercovouni, 4

Merfield, Garland, 107

Metropolis, 129

metropolitan, 114, 123–124, 126–127, 129, 137

Metropolitan Anthony, 114, 123–124, 129

migrate, 8

mistake, 75–76, 115–116, 136

MJB Coffee, 100

Model T Ford, 36

Modesto, 23

Mollie Stone's Tower Market, 61

mom, 19–21, 23–24, 26, 31, 33–34, 36, 64

monastery, 35

Money, 1, 16–17, 20–21, 23, 26, 33, 35, 44–45, 51, 61, 63, 74, 77, 79, 81–83, 86, 93–94, 96, 98–101, 103, 113, 135, 141, 148

Montgomery Street, 72

Morenz, Mark, 144

Moschonas, Loula, 114

mother, viii, 5, 9, 16–17, 19–21, 23, 27, 32, 34, 36, 48, 65, 134, 147

Mr. Chambers, 89

Mr. Daldos, 17

Murray Steeg, 86

music, 61, 69, 105, 121–122, 131, 135, 138

musical instruments, 133

mutual fund industry, 94–95

My Big Fat Greek Wedding, 60

National Investment Marketing Services, 71

National Registry of Unclaimed Retirement Benefits, 99

Native American, 22

naturalization, 10

Neochorion, Tripoli, 4

New York, 8, 19, 58, 82–83, 125

newspaper, 9, 59, 61, 93, 135, 144

Newton, Wayne, 81

NFL Today, 78

Nob Hill, 46

Norman Jr, James R., 97

Norman, Jim, 96–97

Northern California, 69, 128, 130

Northern Conference, 128

NRURB, 99, 101

Oedipus, 3

Okrasinski, Scott, 98

Oli Mazi, 144

Olympic Club, 24, 40, 58

Ontario, 127

opportunity, viii, 25–26, 30, 52–53, 58, 70, 72, 94, 109, 117–119, 123, 135–137, 139, 141, 149

Orange County, 73, 95

Ottoman Empire, 4, 135

Ottoman Turkish government, 20–21

Panagopoulos, Theodore, 4

Panayia, 27

Panayoti, 8, 27

Papangellin, George, 133

Park La Brea, 69

Pascha (Easter), 33

Paterakis sisters, 128

Patras, 19

Paychex, 97

Peloponnese, 4

Peloponnesians, 4

PenChecks, v, 93, 95–99, 101–103

Pennsylvania, 21

pension field, 73, 79, 103

pension industry software, 94

pension plan, 79–80

pension services, 73

performances, 44, 142

Performing Arts Center, Los Angeles, 69

Peros (Simvoulakis), Irene, 134

PERT (Program Evaluation Review Technique), 112

Peterson, Robert O. "Bob", 72–73

Phantom of the Opera, 22

Phillips, Perry, 108

pilot's licenses, 68

Pirovolos, 4, 8

Pitzer, Ann, 107

plan, 401(k), 88, 94, 100

Plato, 3, 105

political awareness, 149

political science, 55–56

politics, 32, 150

Pontics, 118–119

Pontos, 106, 118–119, 138

Portola Drive, 61

Portuguese royalty, 58

possibility thinker, 45, 47–48, 114, 137, 140

Potter Valley, California, 37

Poulos family, 37

Poulos, Father Sam, 128

Poulos, Paul and Pearl, 37–40

Poulos, Paul Jr. and John, 37–40

Poulos, Thomas, 148

prayer, viii, 44, 126

Preovolos, ii, viii, 4, 8, 13–14, 16–17, 19–21, 23, 25, 43, 51, 97, 116, 143

Preovolos, Constantine John (Gus), 8–10, 14, 16–17, 24

Preovolos, George John, 8–10, 14, 16–17, 24

Preovolos, George Theodore, 4

Preovolos, John George, 8

Preovolos, Louis "Troy", 13–14, 17, 23–24

Preovolos, Nicholas, father, 5, 8, 32–35, 43, 51

Preovolos, Nick (son), 69, 143–144

Preovolos, Panayotis (Peter) John, 8, 13, 15–17

Preovolos, Spiro (son), 69, 116

Preovolos, Thanasi (son), 68–69, 124–125

Preovolos, Vaselike (Aunt Bessie), 16–17

Prohibition, 16, 26, 98

Proverbs, 29

Puccinin, Barbara, 97

Rainbow Girls, 44, 46–47

Rains, Claude, 22

Ralston Purina Co., 72

Rather, Dan, 43

Ready Retirement System, 86–87

real estate license, 63, 70

regional costumes, 107

regional dances, 110

registered investment advisors, 95

religion, 30, 32, 147, 149

religious persecution, 35

respectful, 33–34

responsibility, ii, 34–35, 37–38, 44, 47, 57, 61, 68–69, 101, 112, 131, 135–136, 149

restaurant, v, 8–9, 13, 15–17, 22, 25, 31, 37, 72, 148

retirement division, 85

retirement industry, 94

Revell, Emma G., 17

Ridley, Robert W. "Bob", 98

Rigolopoulos, Madelynn, 107

Romania, 110

Rome, 150

Rose Bowl, 108, 139–140

Rose, Pete, 43

Roxanne Cantos, 107

Russia, 34

S&W, 65

Saint Sophia Greek Orthodox Cathedral, 69

San Diego Trust & Savings Bank, 73

San Diego Yacht Club, 71

San Francisco, 8–9, 11, 14–17, 22–25, 30–31, 36, 40, 45–47, 53–55, 58, 61, 64, 67–72, 78–79, 109, 129

San Jose, 24, 118–119

San Mateo, 33

Sansum Medical Clinic, 30

Santa Barbara, 30

Saudi Arabia, 52

saving (importance of), 33

SBA, 86

Scarvelis, George, 107

Scarvelis, Jeanne, 107

SCFNB, 71–73, 75

school, 32–33, 38, 43–44, 48, 51–53, 55–59, 67, 136, 141, 143–144

Schweitzer, Albert, 59, 147

Scott, Willard, 43

Security Pacific National Bank, 70

self-hypnosis, 54

Senior Management Team, 111, 136

Serbia, 110

service clubs, 45, 53

Seven Habits of Highly Effective People, 95

Shanghai, 34

Sheraton, Anaheim, 129

Silberman, 71–73

Silberman, Richard T. "Dick", 71–73

Simmons, Mark, 102

Simos, Barba, 35–36

Sinatra, Frank's daughter, 53

Sirtos, 109

Skouras, Charles, 69

Small Business Administration, 86

Socrates, 3, 105

Sokratis, 19

Souliotes, 135

Southern Arizona Bank and Trust Company, 10

Southern California First National Bank, 71

Southern Pacific Railroad, 62

Spackman, Perry, 62

sports, 80–81, 109, 136

St. John's Greek Orthodox Church, Anaheim, CA, 108

St. Paul, 8

St. Spyridon Annual Food Festival, 139

St. Spyridon Greek Orthodox Church, 106

Stamos, Dena, 134

stamp collecting, 22, 48

Stassis, Tina, 107

Stephen, Peter Randal, 97

Sterling Furniture Co., 16

stockholders, 97

Stockholm, Sweden, 37

Stoller, John, 79

stories, viii, 20–21, 26, 59, 106, 148

Strauss, Levi, 100

student teacher, 56–57

success, v, 2, 13, 15, 17, 47, 59, 63, 90, 102–103, 114, 142

Sunday school, 55

Swig, Ben, 47, 72

Taylor, Elizabeth, 31

team sports, 136

Teamsters, International Brotherhood of, 63–64

teamwork, 110–112, 132, 136

teenager, 44–45, 47, 61, 106, 108, 114, 120

Telegraph Avenue, Oakland, CA, 22

Thanos, A.K., 17

Themis Gallanis, 107

theosis, 111, 151, 161

Thessaloniki, 58, 118–119

third-party administration, 95

third-party administrators, 86, 93, 95

Thomas J. Watson, 13

Thrace, 20–21, 133

Thunderbird International School of Management, 56–57

Touloumis, Emanuel John, 20

Touloumis, Fotini Doris, 19

Tower Market, 61

Townsend Street, 17

TPA, 79, 93–95, 102

trade shows, 86, 97–98

traditional dances of Greece, 106–107

traditions, 106, 148

Trojan War, 4

Trompas, Christine, 107

trust department, 67, 70–71, 73–74, 85, 87, 90–91

Tsamikos, 109

Turkey, 7, 19–21, 110

Turks (Ottomans), 135

Twentieth Century Fox, 69

Twin Peaks, 61

UC Berkeley, 21

Ukiah, 37, 40

uncashed check services, 99

Union Bank, 75, 86

United States, ii

United Way, 45

University of Arizona, 52, 55–56, 59, 141

University of California, Davis, 37

University of California, Hastings College of the Law, 38

Utrecht, The Netherlands, 37

villages, 5, 106, 131, 133

Virgin Mary, 27

Wagner, James, 97

Walker, Yvonne, 97

Wallner, Gary, 128

Walt Disney, 43

Warren, Senator Elizabeth, 102

Washington, DC, 93

Watson, Thomas J., Sr., 13

Wayne, John, 43

wedding, 4, 23, 30, 58, 60, 131

Weil, Dave, 107

Weinreich Jr., Philip H., 97

Weinstein's Department Store, 17

Weinstein, Isadore, 17

Wells Fargo, 45, 67–71, 100, 109

Wert, Charles "Chuck", 73

wife, 3, 16–17, 26, 34, 41, 44, 54, 62, 64, 68, 76–77, 79–80, 83, 108, 126, 140, 143–144, 147

work ethic, 33, 149

World War I, 7, 9–10

World War II, 58

wrestler, 24–25, 40

wrestling, 24, 51

Wright, Jim, 58

writing, ii, vii–viii, 105, 148

yearbook, 51

young adults, 106–107, 109–110, 115, 123, 139

Youth Conference, 128–130

youth group, 106

Zalongo, Dance of, 135

Zebot, Peter, 97

Zigouri, Thanna, 4

Zorba Dancers, 106

LIVING LIFE
TO THE
FULLEST
Ζώντας τη Ζωή στο Έπακρο

A Photo Companion

PETER E. PREOVOLOS

Living Life to the Fullest, A Photo Companion, by Peter E. Preovolos, is a digital compilation of captioned photos, news clippings and historical documents, as well as versions of the Preovolos family tree done by relatives living in the US and abroad.

Visit issuu.com/LivingLifetotheFullest

Made in USA - Kendallville, IN
52965_9781957651040
07.27.2022 0931